THEY LOVED THE LAND

 A TARGET BOOK

THEY LOVED THE LAND

Edited, with commentary
by Bennett Wayne

GARRARD PUBLISHING COMPANY
CHAMPAIGN, ILLINOIS

Library of Congress Cataloging in Publication Data

Wayne, Bennett.
    They loved the land.

    (A Target book)
    SUMMARY: Biographies of four people whose love of
nature inspired them to superior achievements in their
field: Rachel Carson, John Audubon, John Muir, and
Luther Burbank.

    1. Naturalists—Biography—Juvenile literature.
[1. Naturalists] I. Title.

QH26.W38   574'.092'2 [B] [920]   74–915
ISBN 0–8116–4908–3

Picture credits:

Ansel Adams from Magnum: pp. 84, 85, 86, cover
Gene Aherns from Bruce Coleman: p. 87
The American Museum of Natural History: p. 40
Brown Brothers: pp. 47, 89, 107, 115 (both), 119
Chatham College: p. 138
Ed Cooper from National Audubon Society: p. 68
Culver Pictures: p. 82
Billy Davis from Black Star: p. 120 (top)
Erich Hartmann from Magnum Photos: pp. 125, 159, 164
Kit and Max Hunn from National Audubon Society: p. 120 (bottom right)
Ray Hunold of National Audubon Society: p. 121 (top right)
George Komorowski from National Audubon Society: p. 121 (top left)
Louisiana State Library: p. 24
Missouri Historical Society: p. 29
Richard Nairin from National Audubon Society: p. 121 (bottom)
National Audubon Society: pp. 34, 42, 43, 44, 45 (both)
Princeton University Library: p. 21
Laurence P. Pringle from National Audubon Society: p. 120 (bottom left)
Dave Repp from National Audubon Society: p. 122 (bottom)
Gordon S. Smith from National Audubon Society: pp. 123, 152
C. Springmann from Black Star: p. 122 (top)
Story of My Boyhood and Youth by John Muir (New York and Boston:
    Houghton Mifflin and Company, 1913): pp. 55, 58 (both), 73
Andrew Walfish, p. 6
White House Collection: p. 9

Acknowledgments:

The quotation which appears on page 84 is from *This is the
American Earth* by Ansel Adams and Nancy Newhall. Copyright ©
1960 by Sierra Club. Used by permission.

The quotation which appears on page 153 is from *Under the
Sea Wind* by Rachel L. Carson. Copyright 1941 by Rachel L.
Carson; renewed 1969 by Roger Christie. Reprinted by
permission of Oxford University Press, Inc.

7590

Contents

They Loved the Land

Here in the hidden recesses of a western canyon is a band of present-day wanderers. They are exploring the many faces of the American wilderness—the towering mountains, the still forests, the rainbow-hued deserts. They are getting to know the vast country they call home.

Many of these wild places exist today because an earlier generation of Americans loved the land and tried to preserve its beauty for all time to come. This book is about four such people of vision.

John James Audubon wandered in the virgin forests of a young America and, with his paintbrush, immortalized the birds who lived there. John Muir devoted his life to exploring the high Sierras. His crusade to preserve the wilderness led to the establishment of some of America's most beautiful national parks. Luther Burbank's questioning mind and his genius with plants enabled him to take from forest and mountainside the seeds of wild flowers and fruits and to develop them into new "creations." Rachel Carson realized the danger to the environment in the careless use of chemicals and had the courage to sound the alarm.

Each of these Americans, in his own way, made it possible for today's generation to enjoy this country's natural treasures—a wondrous gift to be used carefully and kept intact for Americans still to come.

JOHN JAMES AUDUBON
1785–1851

loved birds and wanted to paint them
even when he was a small boy in
France. His hobby became the most
important thing in his life when he
came to America. Although Audubon
became a storekeeper in Louisville,
Kentucky, he spent little time behind
the counter of his store. Instead, he
roamed the forests surrounding the
frontier village, studying birds and
drawing them. When his business
ventures failed, it became clear to
Audubon that he could not be a
businessman and an artist at the same
time. There were long years of poverty
and separation for Audubon and his
family while he traveled thousands of
miles, carefully recording with brush
and paint the birds of his adopted land.
His paintings captured for all time the
days when America was young, and
virgin forests teemed with beautiful birds
of every description.

John James Audubon
Painter of Birds
by James Sterling Ayars

1. The Book of Birds

Fougère stopped short and peered into a clump of tall grass. There, almost hidden, was a bird's nest. The boy's dark eyes shone as he turned toward his father.

"Look, father!" he exclaimed. "There is a bird's nest, and it has some eggs in it!"

Captain Audubon smiled at the boy. He loved walking with his young son through the countryside around Nantes, a city on the west coast of France. He showed Fougère where to find birds' nests. He told him how birds fly south in autumn and north in spring. The boy listened carefully to everything his father taught him about the wildlife of his new country.

Captain Audubon had lived in Santo Domingo, now known as Haiti, for several years. There Fougère and his sister Rosa had been born, and there Captain Audubon had become a successful merchant. When Fougère's mother died, Captain Audubon returned home to France. Soon afterward, he sent for the two children and introduced them to their new mother,

Anne Audubon. Madame Audubon loved the two children and brought them up as though they were her own.

For a time the small family lived in Nantes, but when the French Revolution broke out, the streets of the city became dangerous. Captain Audubon moved his wife and children to a small village outside Nantes. He himself took command of a ship in the navy of the new French Republic.

Captain Audubon was not home often. When he was, he tried to spend as much time as possible with Fougère. One day when they were walking through the woods, they found some baby birds.

Fougère liked the birds so much that he wanted to take them home with him.

The captain asked, "How could you take them home without killing them?"

Fougère did not know what to say. He wanted to have the birds close to him. But he did not want to kill them.

A short time later, Captain Audubon put a book into Fougère's hands. In the book were many pictures of birds.

Slowly Fougère turned the pages of the book. Suddenly he knew how he could take birds home without killing them. He could draw pictures of them. He could take them home on paper.

"A new life ran in my veins," Fougère wrote many years later, when he was known as John James Audubon, a famous painter of birds.

After that day Fougère went often into the fields and woods to draw pictures of birds. He tried to make each drawing better than the one before.

Captain Audubon and his friends said that Fougère's drawings were very good. Fougère wanted them to be still better.

"These drawings," he said to his father, "make the birds look like a family of cripples."

Before he was fourteen, Fougère had made hundreds of drawings of birds. But he did not think his drawings were good enough to keep. On some of his birthdays, he made bonfires of them.

2. The Museum

Fougère looked about his room with pride. Birds' nests, birds' eggs, plants, and rocks were neatly placed on shelves and tables.

"It makes quite a show," he thought.

While Captain Audubon had been at sea, Fougère had turned his room into a museum. Almost every day, instead of going to school, he had wandered in the fields and woods. Almost every day he had brought back something for his museum.

Now his father was coming home. Fougère would show him the museum.

Footsteps sounded in the hall, and seconds later the captain walked into the room. He looked over the birds' nests, the eggs, the plants, and the rocks.

"Very good! Very good!" he said. Then he asked, "And what have you done in school while I have been so long away?"

Fougère hung his head. He did not answer. Without saying another word, Captain Audubon left the room.

After dinner that evening, the captain asked Rosa to play her violin. Rosa played so well that Captain Audubon gave her a beautiful big book he had brought home.

"Now, Fougère!" the captain said.

Slowly Fougère took his violin out of its case. One of the strings was broken.

The captain looked at his wife.

"He has not been practicing," Madame Audubon said softly.

The captain asked Fougère questions about his school lessons. Fougère could answer only a few of the questions.

"He has not been studying much," Madame Audubon said. She was very kindhearted. She did not make Fougère do what he did not want to do.

13

Captain Audubon had a quick temper. At times it was like a hurricane. But now he did not let it rise. He looked at Madame Audubon. He kissed Rosa. Then, humming a tune, he left the room.

3. Off to Study

When Fougère went to bed that night, he did not go to sleep right away. He lay thinking for a long time.

He knew that his father wanted him to be a sailor or an engineer. He knew that he should not spend so much of his time watching birds. Now that he was fourteen, he ought to be studying arithmetic and geography. These were two things that every sailor and engineer should know. He ought to be studying music, which every French gentleman should know.

Fougère's father wakened him before the sun rose the next morning. Before Fougère knew what was happening, he and his father were sitting in a carriage. His trunk had been loaded in. His violin, in its case, was under his feet.

The driver took his place in the seat ahead. Soon the carriage was rattling through the city streets.

Fougère listened to the clop, clop of the horses' shoes. He wished his father would tell him where they were going and why.

When daylight came, Captain Audubon took a book from one of his pockets and began to read.

Fougère was left to his own thoughts. He remembered some of the things that his father had told him.

"Knowledge and hard work and honesty are more important than money," his father had often said. "Money can be lost in a short time. But knowledge cannot be taken away."

Fougère and his father traveled for several days. Finally they arrived in Rochefort, a seaport city. In front of a big house, the carriage stopped. The house was where Captain Audubon lived when he was in Rochefort on business for the French navy.

Inside the house, Captain Audubon sat down beside Fougère. He took Fougère's hand.

"My beloved boy," he said, "I have brought you here that I may be able to pay constant attention to your studies. You shall have ample time for pleasures. But the remainder *must* be employed with industry and care.

"This day is entirely your own. I must attend to my duties. If you wish to see the docks and the fine warships and walk around the wall, you may accompany me."

For several days, Captain Audubon tried to pay "constant attention" to his son's studies.

Then one day the captain was ordered to go to

England on navy business. Before he left, he put Fougère in the care of his secretary.

Fougère did not like the secretary. He did not like the arithmetic lessons that the secretary gave him. He did not like the room in which he studied. He felt like a prisoner of war.

One day he slipped away from the secretary and jumped from a window into the garden below.

As his feet touched the grass, he felt free. As he walked among the trees, he felt happy again. But he did not feel free or happy for long.

The secretary had seen him jump from the window. He ordered Fougère to be put in the sailors' prison ship in the harbor. There Fougère stayed until his father came back to Rochefort.

Captain Audubon let Fougère out of prison. He scolded his son and promptly sent him back to his studies.

After an unhappy year in Rochefort, Fougère returned to the peaceful village near Nantes. Again he roamed in the fields there. Again he drew pictures of birds. Some of these pictures, he thought, were good enough to keep.

When Fougère was about seventeen, his father sent him to Paris to study drawing. His teacher was Jacques Louis David, a famous French artist.

David wanted his pupils to draw pictures of old

statues. Fougère wanted to draw pictures of living birds.

He was almost as unhappy in Paris as he had been in Rochefort. He stayed in Paris for only a few months. But from David he learned some things about drawing that helped him. Years later he wrote, "David had guided my hand in tracing objects of large size."

4. Off to Mill Grove

At seventeen, Fougère was no longer a boy. He did not like the name Fougère, which means fern. Sometimes people called him *La Forêt,* the forest. More often he was known as Jean Jacques Audubon.

Jean Jacques was old enough to be fighting the British, Captain Audubon thought. The French were at war with the British, and the French navy needed men.

Young Audubon did not want to fight the British or anyone else. But he did what his father wanted him to do. He joined the French navy as a midshipman.

He made one cruise on a man-of-war. But he liked the navy even less than he liked arithmetic. As soon as peace came, he left the navy.

What should the captain do with his son now? Years ago, as a young man, Captain Audubon had fought with the French navy to help the American colonies in the Revolutionary War. He had grown to love the American people and their love of freedom.

Later, while he lived in Santo Domingo, he had visited the new nation and had bought some land there. Now, worried about his son, the captain thought of Mill Grove, his farm near Philadelphia.

Jean Jacques should go to the United States to live on the farm. Maybe he could learn to manage it.

In the fall of 1803, Jean Jacques Audubon boarded a sailing ship bound for New York. He was now eighteen.

He hated to leave his stern but just father. He hated to leave his *chère maman*, kind, plump Madame Audubon. But he wanted to see the United States.

Soon after he landed in New York, he became ill with yellow fever. Luckily, the captain of the sailing ship heard that the young Frenchman was sick. He took him to a boardinghouse a few miles from Philadelphia.

The boardinghouse was kept by two kind Quaker ladies. They took care of young Audubon until he was well. They taught him to speak English.

Like other Quakers of their time, they said "thee" and "thou" instead of "you." For the rest of his life, Audubon often said "thee" and "thou" instead of "you."

At about this time, he began to sign his name John James Audubon. He used the English words for Jean Jacques.

One day Miers Fisher, a Quaker from Philadelphia, came to see young Audubon. Mr. Fisher was an old friend of Captain Audubon's. He had heard that his friend's son had been sick. He took young Audubon to his home.

Mr. Fisher was a "good and learned man." He wanted to be kind to his guest. But he was very strict. He did not like music or dancing, hunting or fishing. Audubon liked all of these things. He was unhappy without them.

"You have cared for me long enough," Audubon said to Mr. Fisher one day. "I am grateful. Now I must go to Mill Grove. It is my father's wish."

Early one morning, Mr. Fisher had his carriage brought to the door. Then he and young Audubon started off to Mill Grove. They arrived just as the sun was setting. In the fading light, Audubon could see orchards, fields with neat fences around them, and a mill beside a stream.

In the big house on the hill, he met William Thomas and his wife. They were taking care of Mill Grove for Captain Audubon. Like Mr. Fisher, the Thomases were Quakers. They warmly welcomed Audubon to his father's house.

John James Audubon was about to begin one of the happiest years of his adventurous life.

"Mill Grove was ever to me a blessed spot," he wrote long afterwards.

5. The Bakewells

It was early spring in the year 1804 when Audubon arrived at Mill Grove. Almost at once he was out in the fields and woods and along the stream. Buds were swelling on the trees, but the air was chilly. Only a few birds had come back from the south.

In the months that followed, Audubon lived a busy life. He painted pictures of birds. He fished and hunted. Each day he found something to bring home. But he did little to manage the farm.

Soon his room looked like a museum. Many birds' eggs, blown out and strung on a string, hung on the walls. Stuffed squirrels, raccoons, and opossums stood on the mantelpiece. Jars of dead fish, frogs, and snakes filled several shelves.

Audubon bought some beautiful horses. He rode one of them whenever he visited the home of a neighbor. He went to many parties and dances.

One of Audubon's near neighbors was William Bakewell, an Englishman. Mr. Bakewell and his family lived on a large farm called Fatland Ford.

"Mr. Bakewell, thy neighbor, called on thee," Mrs. Thomas said one afternoon when Audubon came home from hunting. "Should thee not call on him?"

Audubon did not think he should call on Mr. Bakewell. A young Frenchman whose father had fought the British did not care to know an Englishman.

One day in late autumn, Audubon took his gun and called his dog, Zephyr. Then he set out through the snow to go hunting. Near a grove of fir trees, he

This whippoorwill is believed to be Audubon's earliest bird painting still in existence.

met a stranger with hunting dogs and a gun. The
two men talked about hunting.

The stranger, Audubon learned, was Mr. Bakewell.
Audubon soon decided that Mr. Bakewell was an
Englishman that a young Frenchman could like.

A few days later, Audubon rode over to Fatland
Ford. Mr. Bakewell was not home, but his daughter
Lucy was there. She was sitting quietly by the fire
in the parlor, sewing.

Lucy rose from her chair when Audubon came into
the room.

"Will you sit down?" she asked. "My father is
away, but he should be home soon. He will be happy
to see you."

Lucy sat down again by the fire. Aubudon sat near
her. Lucy talked and sewed.

Audubon talked and looked at Lucy. He liked the
pink in her cheeks. He liked her bright eyes and her
gay talk.

When Mr. Bakewell came home, he seemed glad
to see Audubon. He invited the young Frenchman to
lunch.

As soon as lunch was over, Mr. Bakewell ordered
his guns and dogs to be made ready. Then off he
went with Audubon for another hunt. Audubon wondered as he left if Lucy liked him.

A few days later, Audubon asked Mr. Bakewell

and his family to dinner at Mill Grove. All the Bakewells came.

After dinner, Audubon, Lucy, and Lucy's brothers and sisters went skating on the frozen stream. Audubon was a good skater. He pushed Lucy on a sled over the ice.

Audubon saw Lucy often after that. He taught her to paint. She taught him to speak better English.

In a very short time, Audubon and Lucy decided they wanted to be married.

Mr. Bakewell liked Audubon, but he said that Lucy was too young to be married. She was only sixteen. Besides, Audubon had no money and no land of his own. He had no business. He could not support a wife.

In January, Audubon sailed for France to tell his parents about Lucy.

Captain and Madame Audubon soon decided that Lucy would make a good wife for their son. They said they would help him start a business so that he could marry Lucy.

John James Audubon stayed more than a year at his old home in France. He waited while his father made plans for starting the business. He wandered in the fields and woods as he had done years before. He painted pictures of birds. And always he thought of Lucy.

An early self-portrait of John James Audubon— painter, student of nature, and sometime storekeeper

At last, Audubon said good-bye to his father and mother. For the second time he boarded a sailing ship bound for the United States. With him he had gold his father had given him. He had a business partner, Ferdinand Rozier, who would help him start a store. He had 200 bird paintings he had made for Lucy.

In the summer of 1807, Audubon and Rozier traveled west to open a store in Louisville, Kentucky. The next spring, Audubon made the long journey back to Mill Grove.

He and Lucy had been engaged for more than three long years. Audubon was now 23 years old.

Lucy was 20. Audubon was not yet making enough money to support a wife. But the store in Louisville had been started. The future looked bright.

6. Storekeeper Audubon

Audubon and Lucy were married in the big house at Fatland Ford on April 12, 1808. The next day, they set out in a stagecoach for the village of Louisville.

At Pittsburgh Audubon and Lucy left the stagecoach. There they found many people waiting for boats to take them down the Ohio River. All the boats were going west.

With other people, Audubon and Lucy boarded an ark, a big raft with a cabin built on it. For twelve days the ark floated down the Ohio River. As the river wound between mighty forests, Audubon and Lucy watched the birds along the bank.

At last they reached Louisville, on the south bank of the river. Audubon found his partner, Ferdinand Rozier, busy in the store. The store was doing well.

Lucy liked Louisville because people there were friendly. Audubon liked it because it had a river in front of it and forests close behind. In the river he could catch fish. In the forests he could find birds that he had not seen before.

Rozier was a good storekeeper. He spent most of

his time in the store. Audubon spent most of his time hunting in the forests or drawing pictures of birds. Sometimes Audubon spent several days in the forests without coming home.

Audubon studied the birds closely. He watched them in flight and at rest. He noticed the kinds of plants they perched on and the kinds of food they ate. He saw how they raised their families.

When Audubon drew a picture of a bird, he needed to look at it very closely. So he had to shoot it. Then he fixed it in place with wires. He tried to make it look alive.

One day when Audubon was in the store, a sad-looking stranger walked in. He was a Scotchman named Alexander Wilson. He carried two packages.

Audubon and Rozier watched as Mr. Wilson opened the packages. They gazed in surprise at what they saw. In the packages were bird pictures that Mr. Wilson had drawn.

Mr. Wilson told Audubon he planned to put the pictures into a book as soon as he could get enough orders for it.

Audubon liked the pictures. He started to order a copy of the book, but Rozier stopped him.

"My dear Audubon," Rozier said in French, "what induces you to subscribe to this work? Your drawings are certainly far better."

Maybe Rozier was right, Audubon said to himself. He did not order the book. Instead, he brought out his own pictures for Mr. Wilson to see. The visitor was surprised that a wilderness storekeeper could draw so well. He was not pleased. Perhaps he was jealous.

For a few days, Audubon and Mr. Wilson hunted birds together. They did not like each other. Later, Audubon often thought about Wilson's idea of putting bird pictures into a book.

The year after the Audubons settled in Louisville, their son Victor was born.

Soon, hard times came to the village. People had little money to spend at the store. So, when Victor was just a year old, the Audubons left Louisville. They moved downriver to a place that was later called Henderson.

There, Audubon and Rozier started another store. Again, Audubon hunted and drew pictures of birds while Rozier ran the store.

Finally, Rozier decided to sell his share of the store to Audubon. With Rozier gone, Audubon had little time for hunting and drawing.

The next year, the Audubons' second son, John Woodhouse, was born.

When Victor was eight years old and John was five, Audubon and several friends built a huge mill.

The mill was for grinding wheat and corn and for sawing trees into lumber. It was so big that people came for miles to see it. But it was not a success.

Audubon lost so much money on the mill that he was put in prison for debt. When he came out of prison, he had only his clothes, his gun, his family, and his pictures of birds.

7. Hard Times

After Audubon came out of prison, he and Lucy talked over what he should do. They decided he should stop being part storekeeper and part artist. He should paint even more bird pictures. In a few years he would have enough pictures for a book.

Lucy knew that Aubudon would have to look for new birds to paint. He would have to be away from home for months at a time. For a while Lucy would have to earn money to help support the family.

Audubon's friends said unkind things about him.

But Lucy did not mind what people said. She felt that some day Audubon would be known to the world as a great bird artist. Victor and John agreed.

"My best friends solemnly regarded me as a madman," Audubon wrote a few years later. "My wife and family alone gave me encouragement."

On an October day in 1820, Audubon left his

family in Kentucky and set out on a flatboat for New Orleans. He traveled down the Ohio River and then down the Mississippi River.

Audubon saw many birds he had not seen before. He stopped the flatboat often so that he could paint pictures of them. When he reached New Orleans, he had no money, but he had many paintings of birds.

The next three years were hard ones for the Audubons. Sometimes they were together. More often they were apart. They never had much money.

Lucy helped to support the family by teaching

A crew of flatboatmen. Audubon shared the life of these rugged rivermen on his trip to New Orleans

school. She taught first in a city in southern Ohio. Later, she and the boys moved to Louisiana. There she taught children who lived on cotton and sugar plantations.

Audubon worked hard. Often he worked sixteen hours a day. Often he slept only four hours at night.

He earned money by giving drawing lessons and by painting many pictures of people.

One day Audubon found that 200 of his bird paintings being shipped in a box had been badly damaged. Even this sad accident did not discourage him.

In the autumn of 1823, Audubon decided to go to Philadelphia. There he hoped to find a printer who would make his bird paintings into a book.

He left Lucy and John in Louisiana, at a place called Bayou Sara. He and fourteen-year-old Victor set out for the north. They traveled part way by steamboat, part way on foot, and part way by horse and wagon. Audubon left Victor with relatives in Kentucky. He went alone to Philadelphia.

8. In Search of a Printer

In Philadelphia Audubon met Charles Bonaparte, a nephew of Napoleon, the emperor of France. Young Bonaparte was writing a book on birds. He introduced Audubon to many scientists and artists.

Soon Audubon's bird paintings were hanging in the famous Academy of Natural Sciences. Many people came to see them. Most of the people thought that Audubon's paintings were the most beautiful bird pictures they had ever seen. His pictures had both birds and plants in them. The pictures were life-size and very detailed.

A few of the scientists and artists were jealous of Audubon.

"Why do you put plants in the pictures with your birds?" one of the scientists asked Audubon. "No real scientist would do that."

"I draw birds as I see them in the forests," Audubon said. "I do not draw them as you see them in a museum."

"Audubon is right," young Bonaparte said. "His birds look alive. They are just as we see them in nature."

Audubon could find no printer in Philadelphia good enough to make his pictures into a book.

"You must go to Europe," Bonaparte told him. "There you will find better printers."

Audubon felt discouraged.

He had no money for a trip to Europe. He went to New York City and then up the Hudson River. In the northern forests he hoped to find birds he had never seen before.

All alone in the pathless forests, he thought of young Bonaparte's advice. Yes, he decided, he would take his pictures to Europe. He would have them made into a book called *The Birds of America*. But first he would have to paint still more pictures for the book. Also, he would have to earn money for the trip.

After visiting Niagara Falls, Audubon started toward Louisiana. He arrived at Bayou Sara by steamboat late in the month of November.

Eagerly he told Lucy his plans.

"I will help you," Lucy said. In the fourteen months Audubon had been away, she had saved some money. She had been teaching.

Audubon now went to work to earn still more money. For more than a year he taught French, music, dancing, and drawing. His pupils were boys and girls from the families who lived near Lucy's home at Bayou Sara.

On April 26, 1826, Audubon wrote in his diary: "I left My Beloved Wife Lucy and My Son John Woodhouse on Tuesday afternoon the 26th April, bound to England."

Three weeks and a day later, he and 400 bird pictures were aboard the good ship *Delos*. Seven years had passed since Audubon had gone to prison for debt.

9. A Printer Found

A week after landing in England, Audubon was invited to exhibit his pictures at the Royal Institution in Liverpool. Many people came to the exhibit—413 in one day. Some came to see the pictures. Some came to see John James Audubon.

This American woodsman made them curious. He wore rough clothes, and he let his wavy black hair flow over his shoulders. He rose early, worked late, ate simple food, and took no strong drink.

From Liverpool, Audubon traveled to Edinburgh, Scotland. He was welcomed warmly. When his pictures were shown there, he became the talk of the city.

A Frenchman who saw the pictures wrote: "A magic power transported us into the forests which for so many years this man of genius has trod."

Audubon was invited to dinners, teas, and even breakfasts. He was made a member of famous scientific and art societies.

"My situation in Edinburgh borders on the miraculous," he wrote to Lucy. "I go out to dine at six, seven, or even eight o'clock in the evening, and it is often one or two when the party breaks up. Then painting all day makes my head feel like an immense hornet's-nest."

Audubon's wild turkey cock, the first of his bird paintings printed by W. Home Lizars

One of the first people Audubon met in Edinburgh was W. Home Lizars, a printer.

"I never saw anything like this before," Mr. Lizars said when he saw Audubon's pictures. He agreed to make the pictures into a book called *The Birds of America*.

"Mr. Audubon," he said, "the people here don't know who you are at all, but depend upon it, they *shall* know."

In 1826 making a colored picture book took a long time.

The first of Audubon's pictures that Mr. Lizars printed was the wild turkey cock. The turkey on the paper was as large as the real turkeys in America.

Audubon decided he could not have all of his pictures printed at one time. They cost too much. He would have five made each year. He would take orders for them.

From Edinburgh, Audubon went to London. He was welcomed there also. Many people had parties for him. They admired his pictures. Some of them ordered copies of his book. Even the queen ordered a copy.

Soon Audubon had bad news. Mr. Lizars's workmen had left him.

Audubon began looking for someone in London who would print his pictures. He felt discouraged.

"Oh, how sick I am of London!" he wrote to Lucy.

At last, Audubon met Mr. Robert Havell, Jr. Young Mr. Havell was in the printing business with his father. Robert Havell & Son were even better printers than Mr. Lizars. They said they would print *The Birds of America.*

But Audubon's troubles were not over. The printing of his pictures went slowly. He had very little money. He worked harder than ever. He got up at four o'clock in the morning to paint.

"I painted all day, and sold my work during the

dusky hours of the evening as I walked through the Strand and other streets," he wrote.

Most of the pictures he painted were of birds. Some were of foxes, otters, dogs, and lambs. He painted any picture he thought people would buy.

Some of the people who had promised to buy copies of his *Birds of America* broke their promises. Then Audubon had to leave London to find other people who would order his book.

Three days after Audubon's second Christmas in England, the fifth part of *The Birds of America* came from the printer. "The work pleased me quite," Audubon wrote to Lucy. Twenty-five of the bird pictures had now been printed.

From England, Audubon wrote long letters to Lucy. Many letters began, "My Dearest Friend and Wife." One letter ended, "Good night my Dearest Love and friend." Another ended, "Now Good Night my dearest Lucy. I must put my sore feet in warm water and go to bed. God bless you all."

In one letter, Audubon told Lucy, "Do remember my beloved wife to teach (no matter how unwilling he may be) our Johny the piano and see that his Drawing goes on regularly and well."

Three years after Audubon landed in England, he came back to America.

He spent a year visiting his family and painting

more pictures of birds. Then he went back to London. This time, Lucy went with him.

In London, Audubon found that he had been made a Fellow of the Royal Society. After that, he sometimes wrote his name, "John James Audubon, F.R.S." He was very proud of these letters at the end of his name. They meant that he was one of the great scientists of the world.

10. Success at Last

Audubon and Lucy were very happy. They were in England together. They were no longer poor. Audubon was now famous. But he did not stop working. He started another book.

In the new book, Audubon wrote about the birds he had painted for *The Birds of America.* He told where and how the birds lived. Lucy and a young Scotchman helped him.

When Audubon finished his first book on the lives of the birds, he and Lucy hurried back to the United States.

Audubon needed more pictures for *The Birds of America* that young Mr. Havell was printing. He wanted to visit places in the South and North and West, and paint birds he had not seen before.

With two helpers, Audubon set out for Florida.

On the way, he met John Bachman, a minister who was living in Charleston, South Carolina. Bachman was a scientist as well as a minister. He and Audubon became great friends.

In Florida, Audubon and his helpers waded for days through swamps and salt marshes. The weather was stormy. Once they were almost drowned.

"Where all that is not mud, mud, mud, is sand, sand, sand," Audubon wrote in a letter. He saw only a few new birds.

He hoped to find new birds in other places. With Lucy, Victor, and John, he traveled north along the coast of Maine.

Victor was then 23 years old. John was almost 20. Audubon decided they were old enough to help him.

Both Victor and John could draw, paint, and write very well. From that time on, Victor had charge of the business of printing and selling the books. John went with his father on long trips and helped him collect birds to paint. Both sons helped Audubon paint pictures and write books.

When Audubon went to Labrador, on the rocky eastern coast of Canada, he took John with him. He tried to cure John of his habit of sleeping late by calling him every morning at four.

In Labrador the weather was rainy, and Audubon often worked in damp clothes. On some days he worked for seventeen hours. He complained because his shoulders and fingers grew tired.

At the end of two months in the wild and grand country of Labrador, Audubon had 23 large drawings to add to *The Birds of America.*

In 1838, twelve years after Audubon first sailed for England, *The Birds of America* was finished.

On its 435 pages, it had pictures of 1,065 birds. Every bird was pictured as Audubon had seen it outdoors. Every bird was its real size.

Audubon felt very happy. He and Lucy celebrated by taking a vacation trip in the Highlands of Scotland.

The next year, Audubon's fifth book on the lives of birds was printed. Then Audubon and the Reverend John Bachman began working on books about the four-footed animals of North America.

Audubon did not like to live in a city. He bought a small farm on the east bank of the Hudson River. It was north of the New York City of his time. He called it "Minnie's Land," in honor of Lucy. "Minnie" is a Scottish word for mother.

There Audubon built a large house. It was near the present 155th Street of New York City. There he spent most of the rest of his life. He took trips to England and Scotland and to far places in the United States. But he always returned joyfully to Minnie's Land.

John James Audubon was a successful artist when his sons Victor and John painted this portrait of him in the wilderness he loved.

Audubon had long wanted to see the Far West. When he was 58 years old, he and four friends traveled hundreds of miles up the Missouri River.

Once Audubon wrote in his notebook: "Buffaloes all over the prairies. The roaring can be heard for miles."

He was nearly gored by a wild buffalo that had been wounded.

Audubon saw some animals he had never seen before. He painted pictures of many of them. Later some of the pictures were printed in the books on four-footed animals.

The trip to the Far West was the last great journey for the great traveler.

Audubon spent the rest of his life quietly with Lucy at Minnie's Land.

His sons, Victor and John, lived with their families in big houses nearby.

Several years after Audubon died, a stone monument in memory of him was put up in a churchyard. It was near Minnie's Land. But people do not need a stone monument to remind them of Audubon. His true and most lasting monument is *The Birds of America*, which all the world loves and admires.

Audubon was a man who knew what he wanted to do. He believed he could do it. With Lucy's help, he did it.

A Portfolio of Audubon Birds

John James Audubon, the great American painter, recorded in *The Birds of America* the countless varieties of birds that live in North America. Here are just a few of the 435 engravings of his watercolors that appeared in the original edition, published during the years 1827–1838.

The AMERICAN BRANT (below) lives mostly in the coastal bays of the Arctic regions of North America. It is related to the Canada Goose and, like this bird, flies south in the winter.

The NIGHTHAWK (right) can be found in the open country and cities of a vast area from the Yukon and Newfoundland to Mexico and Florida.

Passenger Pigeon

Audubon described in 1813 a vast migration of
PASSENGER PIGEONS in Kentucky that took three
days to pass. Yet this wild bird, which was found in
large numbers in the eastern part of North America
in the 1800s, had been completely wiped out at the
end of the century by greedy hunters.

The RUFFED GROUSE is a short-tailed brown bird that lives in the woods, usually near trails and clearings, in an area extending from Alaska and Nova Scotia to Colorado and Alabama.

Fork-tail Petrel
THALASSIDROMA LEACHII

LEACH'S PETREL is a small, fork-tailed bird that lives offshore on both the North Atlantic and North Pacific oceans. It skims the waves on sharp, pointed wings and finds shelter from storms in the lee of passing ships.

JOHN MUIR
1838–1914

was never so happy as when he was exploring the dense forests and the towering mountains of the American wilderness. Alone, on foot, and without a gun, he tramped through state after state, taking notes in his journal and stopping only long enough to earn a little money. "I have chosen the lonely way," he said, and he traveled it joyfully. In California, John fell in love with the rugged high Sierras and the beautiful Yosemite Valley. He roamed through their wild and lonely places and made them his home. John Muir spent the rest of his life exploring and studying the Sierras and fighting for their survival in their natural state. His determination and his persuasive writings helped save these untamed lands and others for the entire nation. America's national parks are today both a national heritage and a monument to the man who fought so fiercely for them.

John Muir

Protector of the Wilderness

by Margaret Goff Clark

1. No More School

It was a cold February night in 1849. John Muir and his younger brother David sat beside the fire at Grandfather Gilrye's house. Almost every night the boys came here to do their homework. Grandfather lived across the street from the Muirs in the little town of Dunbar, Scotland, on the North Sea.

All at once the door flew open. Father stood there, his eyes shining.

John almost dropped the little cake he was eating. Although his father and mother and their seven children lived nearby, father never came here. He and grandfather did not like each other.

"Put away your books and come home!" cried father. "Tomorrow we're going to leave for America!"

John jumped up. "We're going! We're really going!" For a long time father had been making plans to go to America to live. Now the time had come.

"Father says he'll buy us a pony when we get there," David shouted.

Grandfather looked sad.

Tears were in grandmother's eyes. "America is so far away," she said. "When will we see you again?"

"We'll come back to visit," said John. "We'll tell you all about the new kinds of birds and flowers that we see."

"We learned all about America in school," said David. "They say there's gold in the ground."

"Maybe we won't have to go to school anymore," John added.

Grandfather shook his head. "Poor boys. You'll find more than flowers and birds and gold in America. Even if you don't go to school, you'll find plenty of hard work."

He went to his bedroom. When he came out he had a gold coin for each of the boys.

Early the next morning, everyone in the family went to the train station. Grandfather and Grandmother Gilrye went, too.

Only father, eleven-year-old John, nine-year-old David, and thirteen-year-old Sarah were going to leave. Mother would stay in Scotland with John's oldest sister, Margaret, and the three youngest children.

John walked beside his mother. "I wish you were coming too," he said.

"I'll be coming soon, Johnnie." She smoothed his unruly red-brown hair one last time. Then she took his hand tightly in her own. "I'll come as soon as father builds a house. I can't take the little ones to such a wild land until we have a home there."

It was late that night when father, John, David, and Sarah sailed from Glasgow harbor. For six weeks they were on the ocean. When they finally reached America, spring had come. But their journey was not over. They had to travel from New York to Wisconsin, where their new home would be.

They went by boat up the Hudson River to Albany, then on the Erie Canal to the Great Lakes. They sailed on the lakes past wild land, farms, and cities to Milwaukee, Wisconsin.

After the boat reached Milwaukee, the Muirs still had to travel by wagon with their clothes and tools and furniture more than 100 miles. Often father and the boys had to push the wagon out of mudholes in the narrow dirt road.

Finally the long trip was over. Father bought a piece of land to farm. Then he started to build a little cabin. Until the cabin was finished, John, David, and Sarah stayed in rented rooms.

One sunny May morning Mr. Muir and the children moved to their new cabin. As the wagon reached the top of a hill, father called, "Look now! There's our farm!"

John wasn't listening to his father. He was looking at a bird with bright blue feathers. It flew to a nest in a tall tree.

The children jumped down from the wagon. John called to David. "A bird! Look at that bird!" To John, every bird was a friend.

He ran to the tree and began to climb. Soon he reached the nest. The bird flew away, and John could see three green eggs.

David was right behind him. "Don't touch the eggs, Davie," said John. "If you do, the mother bird won't come back. Then the eggs will never hatch."

John climbed higher in the tree and looked around. He could see the tiny house where they would live until father built a bigger one. Below the hill was a meadow full of bright flowers, and at the edge of the meadow was a lake.

Suddenly, John wanted to fly like the strange blue bird he had seen. This was a wonderful place, and he was happy. Soon they would have a pony to ride. Father had promised, and he never went back on a promise.

2. A Pony Named Jack

Father kept his word. One day when he came home from town, he was leading an Indian pony.

"Here's your pony," he said. "His name is Jack."

John, David, and Sarah ran happily around the pony.

"He looks strong," said John.

"Why, he's the same color as your hair," Sarah told John.

It was true. The pony was red-brown, except for his black mane and tail.

John was the first to ride the pony. He had to ride bareback, for there was no saddle. He hung onto the pony's black mane to keep from falling. When he wanted to stop, he cried, "Whoa!"

The pony stopped so suddenly that John flew over his head.

But John wasn't hurt. He climbed onto the pony again. Day after day he practiced, until he was a good rider.

But there was not much time to ride Jack or play on Fountain Lake Farm. Father hired a man to help him clear the land. They sawed down trees and cut them up for fences and firewood.

John and David piled up the small branches and bushes and burned them.

Sarah cooked the meals, cleaned the house, and mended the clothes. She and John did the washing.

The children didn't go to school, but father made them learn Bible verses every day. If they forgot the words, he whipped them.

John was learning other lessons too. He watched the birds and animals and studied how they lived.

One of the birds John liked best was the black and white kingbird. One day he watched a little kingbird chase away a big hawk that came to rob its nest. The kingbird followed the hawk into the air. It dived onto the hawk's back and hit the big bird with its sharp bill. The hawk flew away as fast as it could.

"The kingbird is a brave fighter," John told David. "It will risk its life to save its babies."

That fall, as soon as the big house was finished, mother and the rest of the children came from Scotland. Now Fountain Lake Farm was really home. John, David, and Sarah happily led their brother and sisters from place to place on the farm and showed them everything.

The Muir children liked the ducks on the pond and the strong oxen that pulled the plow. But they liked Jack, the pony, best of all.

John and David took turns riding the pony to bring in the cows. Jack knew when it was time to go. If John or David was late, Jack went out by himself.

The pony would chase the cows from the meadow to the barn. This made father angry. He said running wasn't good for the cows.

One night when Jack chased the cows down the lane, father called to John, "Get the gun and shoot Jack."

John begged his father to change his mind. "I'm sorry I was late getting the cows," he said. "Please don't make me kill Jack."

Finally father said, "All right, but I'm going to sell him."

John knew he would never see the pony again.

3. John Digs a Well

All the Muirs worked hard to make their farm a success. But after six years of farming, father decided that the family should move.

He bought more land a few miles away. Then the family left Fountain Lake and moved to Hickory Hill. Again the Muirs had to clear land for farming. John, now seventeen, had to give up hope of going to school.

There were no good lakes or streams on the new farmland. A well had to be dug. Father told John that he was to do it.

It was easy to dig the first ten feet, but then John hit sandstone.

"You'll have to chip out the rock," father told him. So John climbed down into the hole. With a hammer and chisel, he began to chip the sandstone. It was hard, slow work. The hole was only three feet wide, so he couldn't stretch out his legs.

Day after day John worked in the well. It got deeper and deeper. Soon father and David had to lower John into the hole in a pail. They pulled him out at noon for dinner, and again at supper time.

John worked in the hole for months. He had dug 80 feet down, but still had not reached water.

One morning John rode down in the big pail. When he got out at the bottom, he started to pick

A drawing of Hickory Hill Farm by John Muir

up the chips of rock he had cut the day before. Suddenly he felt weak. He could not stand up.

He could hear his father calling, "What's the matter, John?"

John could not answer. He stared up at the round piece of sky at the top of the hole. He saw the branch of an oak tree high above. Then he felt a little stronger, for he loved trees.

"Take me out," he said softly.

"Get into the pail!" father shouted.

John crawled into the pail.

Father and David pulled him out as quickly as they could. John took deep breaths of air.

He was sick for days. A neighbor, who had once been a miner, came to see him.

"There was poisonous gas in the bottom of the hole," he told John. "I have seen coal miners die from that same gas. You're lucky to be alive."

The miner told father how to get rid of the gas. "Tie some hay onto a rope," he said. "Drop the hay into the hole, and pull it up and down. That will carry good air to the bottom of the hole."

As soon as John was better, he went down into the hole again. When the well was 90 feet deep, John finally came to water. It was good, pure water. That was a joyful day for the Muirs, and most of all for John.

4. A Strange Alarm Clock

Every evening after supper and Bible study, John sat down to read. He had only a few minutes to read before going to bed. He loved books. There were so many things he wanted to learn. He longed to go to school, but he was still needed to work on the farm.

One winter evening, father said, "Go to bed, John. This is the second time I've told you."

With a sigh John closed his book.

Then his father said, "If you *must* read, get up early in the morning. Get up as early as you wish."

The next morning John woke up very early. It was only one o'clock! It was too cold to sit and read, so he tiptoed down to the cellar. He would begin to work on an invention. John often thought about things he would like to make, but he had never before had the time. He knew what he wanted to make first: a small, self-starting sawmill.

There was wood in the cellar, and there were a few tools. John started to work at once.

Father wasn't happy about the noise John made, but he didn't stop him from getting up early. After all, he had given his word. He wouldn't break it.

Every day from then on, John got up at one in the morning and worked on his invention.

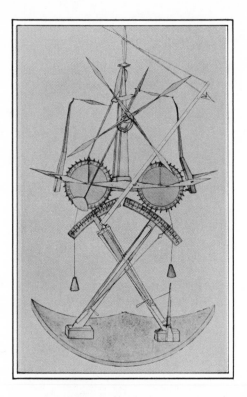

John Muir's drawings of two boyhood inventions: a combination barometer and thermometer (left) and a self-starting saw-mill (below)

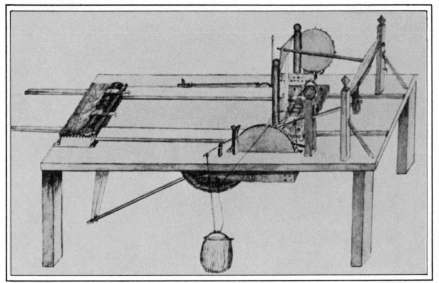

When the sawmill was finished, he set it up beside a stream. It started and began to cut wood just like a big sawmill. "It works!" John shouted.

His mother looked at the sawmill and said, "I'm proud of you, son." Mother always understood and was kind.

Next John made a clock. It told the day of the week and the day of the month. It struck the hours.

It was also a kind of alarm clock. It could start machinery that tipped a bed and rolled the sleeper onto the floor. John called it an "early-rising machine."

Many of the neighbors heard about John's inventions. They came from miles around to see the things he had made.

"You're a fine inventor," one man told him.

"I could do more if I had an education," John answered. "I'd like to find a job in a factory or machine shop. Then I could earn some money for school."

"Why don't you take your inventions to the State Fair in Madison?" the man asked. "Someone who likes your work might hire you."

Madison was the capital of Wisconsin. John would have to take a train to get there. It seemed like a long trip, but John knew that the University of Wisconsin was in Madison. Perhaps he could go to school there.

John thought for a minute. Then he smiled at the man. "I think you have a good idea. I will go to the fair. Thank you, sir!"

5. The Outdoor Class

"Father, I'm going to the State Fair," John said one day. "I hope to find a job in Madison."

Father looked cross. "You should stay at home and help me."

John shook his head. "I'm 22 years old now. The younger boys can help you. I've never liked farming. I want to be on my own."

That day, John left for Madison. He had in his pocket about fifteen dollars: the gold piece his grandfather had given him long ago plus a little money he had managed to earn. His father would not give him any money.

At the State Fair many people saw John's inventions. Crowds watched his early-rising machine. Two boys took turns lying on a small bed. Everyone laughed when the bed tipped and slid the boys onto the floor.

John won a prize of fifteen dollars for his inventions.

When the fair was over, John worked at odd jobs so he could stay in Madison. He often walked on the university grounds. He wanted so much to go to school there.

One day he saw a student he had met at the fair. They stopped to talk.

"You don't need much money to go to school here," the student told John. "I live on bread and milk. You could, too."

John went to see the head of the university. John told him that he had not had many years in school, but he had read a great deal. After some tests, he was told that he could enter the university.

John was happy to be in school once again. He liked the other students and they liked him.

John's favorite class was geology. Geology is the study of the earth and how it was made.

"Our class will meet outdoors," said the teacher, Professor Carr. "That's the best way to learn about the earth."

The class members walked in fields. They climbed hills and walked beside lakes.

"Thousands of years ago a glacier moved across this land," said Professor Carr. "A glacier is a river of ice. These glaciers moved slowly over the ground. They dug out valleys and sometimes made lakes."

John's blue eyes were shining. Glaciers! So they had helped to shape the earth! He wanted to know more.

John went to the library that night. He found some books on glaciers. After he had read them, Professor Carr let John borrow some of his own books.

John liked English class, too. His teacher told him to keep a notebook. "Write down your thoughts and ideas. Make notes about things you see and do," the teacher said.

John did well in school, but he was often hungry. He was so busy with his lessons he didn't have much chance to earn money for food. One time he became sick because he lived for days on crackers and water.

At last his father sent him some money. John was glad he could eat again. He was even more pleased to know his father cared about him.

During the summers John did farm work to earn money for his next year at school.

One June day a small thing happened, but it changed his life. He stopped to talk with a friend, Milton Griswold. Milton told John about his favorite class. It was botany, the study of plants. John became so interested he bought a botany book. He found out he liked botany, too.

Now Milton and John spent many hours in the woods and fields. They found plants and read about them in their books. A new, exciting world was opened to John.

6. Blind!

In the spring of 1863, John made plans to go to medical school in the fall. But after a summer of hiking and exploring, he decided to wait before studying medicine.

"I want to make the woods and fields my school for now," John said. One day he put some things he would need into a small backpack and started off.

For weeks he hiked through one state after another. He even hiked into Canada. John studied the different plants he found. He made notes.

Sometimes he traveled with a friend and sometimes he was alone. When he ran out of money, he found a job. One job was in Indianapolis, Indiana. There he worked in a wagon factory.

The first week, John earned $10. He did such good work he earned $18 the second week. Before long he invented a way to make better wagon wheels and to make them more quickly. The factory owner raised his pay to $25 a week, good pay for those days.

One day John was working late at the factory. He was using a sharp file. As he bent over a machine, the file slipped. The point went into his right eye, and John was blinded. He was taken to a doctor, who said nothing could be done to bring back John's sight.

For almost a week John lay in bed. His left eye was now also blind. Friends came and tried to comfort him. The boys from his Sunday school class read to him. But John could think only of his terrible loss.

One day a friend brought an eye doctor to see John. This doctor checked both of John's eyes. "Your right eye will get better with time. Then you will be able to see with your left eye, also. It only became blind in sympathy with the right eye. You will see almost as well as ever, but you must rest for now."

How happy this made John!

The owners of the wagon factory asked him to come back to work. They said he would soon be made a partner in the company.

"No, thank you," said John. "I want to use my eyes to study the woods and fields and mountains." Years later John told a friend, "I might have been a millionaire, but I chose to become a tramp."

As soon as his eyes were well, he went home to see his mother and father and brothers and sisters.

"I'm going to take a long nature hike," he told them. "I'll be gone for many months."

He gave his brother David some money that he had earned in the wagon factory.

"Will you keep this for me?" he asked. "I'll let you know where to send it when I need it. I don't want to carry much money with me."

7. Robber on Horseback

When John left his home, he traveled by train and by raft to Jeffersonville, Indiana. Then he started off on foot. John was 29 years old. He was going to hike through the South until he reached the Gulf of Mexico. Before the journey was over, he would walk about a thousand miles.

He wore a pack on his back and carried his plant press. The press would hold the flowers he found.

John stayed away from cities. He wandered through fields and over mountains. He looked for plants and flowers new to him. He picked every new flower he saw and put it into his plant press. How wonderful it was to be enjoying nature once again!

John often thought about how he would spend the rest of his life. He knew he could not make a living hiking across the country and looking at flowers. Perhaps he could write nature books, he thought. So every day he made notes about the things he saw.

One day as John hiked through mountains in Tennessee, a man on horseback came up to him.

"I'll carry your pack for you," said the man.

"No, thank you," said John. "It's not heavy." He had a feeling the horseman was a robber.

"Give me the pack," the man said. Without a word, John gave it to him.

As soon as the horseman had it, he rode ahead.

John walked after him as fast he could. "I guess I won't see my pack again," he thought.

As John came around a bend in the path, he saw the horseman. The man had opened the pack.

When he saw John, he closed the pack and gave it to him. "Here you are," said the horseman.

John put the pack on his back. He walked on, smiling to himself. How sad the robber must have been to find no money in the pack. It held only a comb and brush, some clean clothes, a towel, soap, and three books.

Some time before, John had written to David. He had asked him to send some money to Savannah, Georgia. But when he arrived no money was waiting for him. John had only one dollar and a half left.

He bought some crackers. He decided to sleep in a graveyard because no robbers would go there. The air was hot and damp, and mosquitoes kept him awake most of the night. He could find only dirty water in a stream to drink.

His money came a week later. Then John took a boat to Florida. There he found many strange flowers to study, but he soon became ill with malaria.

For a long time John lay sick in bed. He was afraid he would never lose his fever in the warm South. He needed cold mountain air.

He remembered pictures he had seen of the Sierra Nevada, a mountain range in California. "I think I could get well there," he thought.

Before long he was on a boat again. He sailed first to Cuba and then to New York. A few weeks later he found a ship bound for San Francisco, California. He was on his way to the Sierras!

8. The Beautiful Valley

John Muir stood on the busy San Francisco dock. He looked up at the city that stood on a hill. It was beautiful, but John didn't want to stay in any city.

He wanted to reach the Sierra Nevada mountain range. He hiked east over hills. He hiked across a wide valley that was full of flowers. The April air felt good on his face.

John could see the mountains miles and miles ahead. The snow shining on their peaks seemed to be a guide light showing him the way. Already his fever was better.

John had once seen pictures of a wonderful valley that was in these mountains. The valley was called Yosemite. Beautiful, high cliffs rose on either side of the valley. John longed to see them.

When at last John came to the Yosemite Valley,

he thought it was even more beautiful than the pictures. He wished he could stay there the rest of his life.

But John's money was running low, so he left the valley to find a job. He worked on a farm for a while. Then he found a job he liked better on a ranch.

In the spring of 1869, John was asked to take a flock of sheep high into the mountains, where there was better grass. That was where John Muir wanted most to go.

So on June 3, he started into the Sierra Nevada with the flock.

The sheep walked slowly, but John didn't care. He wanted to see as much of the mountains as he could.

One morning in July John found some rocks that were different from the others in that part of the mountains.

"How did they get here?" he asked himself.

Then he saw long scratches on some of the rock walls. He had seen marks like that on the rocks near Madison, Wisconsin. Professor Carr had said they were made by glaciers.

That's how the strange rocks got there! Glaciers had brought them. A great river of ice had come from the north thousands of years ago. The glacier had made the marks on the rocks, too.

Breathtaking Vernal Falls in John Muir's beloved Yosemite Valley still overwhelms adventurous travelers today.

John wrote his thoughts about the glacier in his notebook.

At last John and the sheep reached the high rim of the Yosemite Valley. From a cliff nearby, John could see the whole valley. It was seven miles long and full of flowers and trees. A shining river ran through it.

John walked as close to the edge of the cliff as he dared. He knew that if the ground under him broke, he would fall thousands of feet, but he had to see it all.

Not far below him was the Yosemite Creek. It poured down over the cliff in a waterfall nine times as high as Niagara Falls.

To get an even better view, John climbed partway down the dangerous, steep cliff. There he stood on a small rock shelf above the falls.

Now he could look straight down into the white water. He could see it splash and spray far below him. For a long time John stayed on the cliff and watched the waterfall. Now he was so happy he forgot to be afraid. Later, he couldn't even remember how he climbed to the top again.

When the summer was over, John took the sheep to their owner. Then he again climbed to Yosemite. This time he found a job working for a man who had built a hotel in the valley. The man had written articles about Yosemite. People who came to see the valley stayed in his hotel.

John's job was to build a sawmill beside Yosemite Creek. The sawmill would cut trees into boards. Then from the lumber John would build more rooms onto the hotel.

In his mill he would use only trees that had blown down. He would not cut down any of the living trees.

John built a big sawmill. It was like the small one he had invented when he was a boy.

Near the creek John built himself a cabin. He used flat stones from the creek bed for the fireplace and the cabin floor. He left cracks between some of the stones on the floor so ferns could grow there. A little brook flowed through one corner of the room.

There was one window, and it looked out on Yosemite Falls. John hung his hammock facing the window. Lying there at night he could hear the falls and watch them too. John was happier than he had ever been before.

9. Save the Wild Lands!

John worked hard at the sawmill. When he had saved some money, he stopped working. He wanted to spend all his time studying the mountains.

He was sure the Yosemite and many other valleys had been formed by glaciers. Some people did not agree. John set out to prove that his theory was right.

He followed the trail of the glacier that he thought had once filled Yosemite. In deep canyons he found the marks left by the glacier.

He wrote an article called "The Death of a Glacier" about his glacier hunt. A New York City newspaper bought the article, and many readers became interested in glaciers. John thought once again about writing books. Maybe he really could earn a living writing about nature.

One day while he was climbing high in the mountains, he found a living glacier. He thought people would have to believe him now.

Still, not everyone did. It was not until years later that people realized that John Muir had been right. Glaciers had helped to shape Yosemite and many other valleys in the Sierra Nevada mountains.

During his climbs in the mountains, John was sorry to see that men were cutting down some of the best forest trees. Then too, sheep were eating all the grass and flowers in the meadows. Now he had another reason for writing articles.

John had been living in the Yosemite Valley for about seven years. In 1875 he came down from the

John Muir—naturalist, author, and protector of the wilderness

mountains to live in San Francisco. His life work would now be to protect the land he loved so much.

"We must save these mountains for our children," he wrote.

John wrote many articles. Thousands of people read them, and he became well known. People began asking him to give talks, but he always said no, thank you.

Then one day John was asked to speak in Sacramento, the capital of California. Many lawmakers lived there. If John spoke to the lawmakers, perhaps he could make them think as he did. Then they would make laws to protect the mountains forever.

This time he said, "Yes, I'll speak."

One of John's friends was an artist who had painted many pictures of the mountains. He knew John was nervous about making the speech. The artist said, "Take one of my paintings with you. You can look at it and think you are in the mountains."

"Thank you," said John. "I'll do that."

John stood up before the rows of people. He couldn't remember what he wanted to say. Then he looked at the painting of the mountains—the mountains he wanted to protect. He was no longer afraid. He talked to the people as if he were sitting with them around a campfire.

Afterward a newspaper article said that John Muir was the best speaker the people of Sacramento had ever heard.

Now everyone who knew about John wanted him to speak to them. He no longer said no.

John kept on writing too. He could reach even more people with magazine and newspaper articles than he could by talking.

In San Francisco John met a young woman named Louie Strentzel. She was different from other girls John had met. She understood how he felt about the mountains. She knew how much he cared about nature.

John kept on hiking in the mountains he loved. He wrote more articles. He even went to Alaska to study glaciers there. But he didn't forget the girl with the dark hair and the gray eyes.

A few months after he came home from Alaska, he and Louie Strentzel were married. John was almost 42 years old.

After their marriage, Louie's father, a fruit grower, gave John and Louie a big piece of land. Grapes and other fruit were growing on it.

John worked for three and a half months on the fruit farm. Then he left again for Alaska. Louie understood that he must go. Alaska had many large glaciers like the one that had helped to make the Yosemite Valley. It was important for John to study them.

10. Stickeen

When John Muir reached Alaska, he packed a big canoe for his trip up the coast. He put in tents, blankets, and food. He hired some Indians to paddle the canoe and help run the camp.

The canoe was ready, but John had to wait for a friend, the Reverend S. Hall Young. At last Mr. Young came. With him was a small black dog. The dog, named Stickeen, jumped into the canoe. He curled up on a blanket.

John looked at him. "I like dogs," he told Mr. Young. "But Stickeen is so small, he'll need a lot of care."

"Oh, no," said Mr. Young. "Stickeen is stronger than he looks. Wait and see. He's a good dog."

Stickeen slept most of the day. When the canoe went toward shore that afternoon, Stickeen jumped into the water. He swam to shore. There he shook himself and waited for the others.

The Indians set up tents and started a fire. John walked into the woods to look for plant life. He heard a small sound behind him. When he turned around, there was Stickeen! Stickeen followed John everywhere. John liked the little dog.

One day Stickeen followed John across a glacier. The ice was so rough it cut the little dog's feet. Soon John saw blood on the ice. He tore up his handkerchief and used it to wrap Stickeen's feet.

One night the Indians set up camp near a large glacier. The next morning John got up early. The wind was blowing. A cold rain was falling.

John did not care, for he liked storms. This was a good day to study the glacier, he thought. He didn't take time for breakfast. Putting a piece of bread into his pocket, he started for the glacier. In his belt was his ice ax.

Soon he looked back. Stickeen was following him. His coat was wet, and his tail was like a string.

John stopped. "Don't come, Stickeen!" he shouted. "This storm is too much for you."

Stickeen did not move. At last John said, "Well, come on if you must." He gave the dog a piece of his bread.

They walked for miles through the rain. At last the sun came out. John and Stickeen walked across the glacier. Then they went far to the north. Sometimes they had to jump across wide cracks in the ice.

John always tried to be careful about jumping. Some of the cracks were deep. If he fell he might break a leg or drop to his death. Stickeen didn't stop to look. He seemed to fly across the wide cracks.

John and Stickeen ate the rest of the bread. It was now afternoon, and they had to turn back. John wanted to reach camp before dark.

Snow began to fall. In the storm John lost his way. He and Stickeen came to many wide cracks which they had to jump across.

Then they came to a crack too wide to jump. John could not find any way around it. He thought about going back, but then they would have to spend the night on the glacier. They might freeze to death.

John saw a narrow ice bridge across the crack. It was ten feet below the spot where they stood.

With his ice ax John cut steps down to the little bridge. The ice bridge was thin. Would it hold him?

John sat down on the bridge and slowly pulled himself across. As he moved, he made the top of the bridge flatter with his ice ax so Stickeen could follow him.

On the other side John made steps in the ice wall so he could climb out.

As soon as he was safe, he called, "Come, Stickeen!"

Stickeen howled. John didn't blame him for being afraid.

"Come on," he said. "You can do it."

At last Stickeen put his paws onto the first step. He went down slowly. Then he started across the ice bridge. It was only four inches wide. If he slipped, he would fall hundreds of feet down into the crack.

John talked quietly to him. "Easy, Stickeen. That's it. You can do it."

Stickeen came across the bridge one careful step at a time. When he reached the other side, he stopped. John was afraid Stickeen could not get up the steep wall. He knew that dogs are poor climbers.

He reached down as far as he could, but Stickeen didn't need help. He almost flew up the steps.

At the top the dog went wild. He jumped into the air. He rolled on the ice. He kissed John's face. Stickeen had always been a quiet little dog. Now he barked and barked.

Hours later John and Stickeen walked into camp.

They were hungry, but they were too tired to eat very much.

John told Mr. Young, "You were right. Stickeen is a brave dog."

11. Maker of Parks

John and Louie were happy to see each other when John returned home from Alaska. John told Louie all about Stickeen. Later he wrote a book about him. He wanted to tell everyone about the bravest dog he had ever known.

In the years that followed, Louie and John had two daughters. They named them Wanda and Helen.

John loved to be with his two girls. When they were old enough, he took them on long walks into the hills near the fruit farm. He told them the names of all the flowers and trees.

Wanda and Helen liked to go to their father's study, where he wrote his articles and books and speeches. The walls were lined with books. There were papers on the desk and on many of the chairs.

One time when Wanda and Helen come up to the study, John was sitting by the wide-open window. "Come here, girls," he said. He took three-year-old Helen on his lap. Wanda, who was eight, leaned against his knee.

"We're going to feed our friends, the birds," John told them. He tied a piece of bread to the end of a long string. With this he coaxed a bird to come from a nearby tree branch to the windowsill.

Besides his writing, John worked hard on the farm. In ten years he had saved enough money to take care of his wife and daughters for life.

Once a year he made a trip to the mountains he loved. Each time he went back to Yosemite, John saw that more of the fine old trees had been cut down. Meadows, once full of flowers, had been turned into hay fields.

One year when he came home from a trip to Yosemite, John told his wife what was happening.

"My friend Robert Johnson and I are going to try to have the Yosemite Valley and the land around it made into a national park," said John. "I'll write articles about it. Robert Johnson will print them in his magazine."

Lumbermen, sheepmen, and cattlemen fought John's plan. The lumbermen wanted to go on cutting the big trees. The sheepmen and cattlemen wanted their animals to feed on the meadows.

But finally John won. Many people had become interested in keeping Yosemite natural, wild country. On October 1, 1890, a new law made Yosemite a national park.

John knew there were other wild lands that should be made into parks. He hired his brother David and another man to run the family farm. Now he was free to work all the time to protect the mountains he loved.

Using the notes he had written on his trips, John wrote books and articles. His first book, *The Mountains of California*, made people all over the country want to save the forests.

John also helped start the Sierra Club. Today, club members still work at protecting the wilderness.

In 1901 Theodore Roosevelt became president of the United States. He had read many of John Muir's books and articles. He had always believed that the wild lands must be saved.

About two years later the president wanted to visit the West. He asked John Muir to take him on a camping trip.

John showed President Roosevelt's letter to Louie. "At last I can talk to a man who will really *do* something about saving our forests!"

The president had many people with him on his western trip. But he and John Muir rode off alone on horseback.

That night they lay down on beds of fir branches and ferns. They talked and talked. John told President Roosevelt about his many trips into the mountains.

President Roosevelt and John Muir together in the
mountains they both loved

"The trees store water, and their roots hold the soil," John told the president. "If many trees are cut down, we will have floods. The soil will wash away. If we don't save our forests now, it will be too late."

For three days and nights, John Muir and President Roosevelt talked and camped together. When they said good-bye, the president said, "Come and see me in Washington. I've had the time of my life!"

During his years as president, Theodore Roosevelt set aside thousands of acres of forests and set up many national parks. He had listened well to John Muir.

Until the day he died in 1914, John never stopped writing about the forests and mountains.

Of course he didn't always succeed in saving the wild lands he loved. John tried to have the beautiful Hetch Hetchy Valley in California set aside as a park like Yosemite. Instead, it was made into a reservoir for San Francisco.

This almost broke John's heart, but he went on working to save other land for people to enjoy. Because of him, we can today visit Yosemite, Sequoia, and Grand Canyon, and many other national parks.

John lived his life in the belief that the trees and flowers, the insects and animals and birds "all are our brothers." He was one of the best friends nature has ever had.

John Muir's Legacy:

America's National Parks

This, as citizens, we all inherit. This is ours, to love and live upon, and use wisely down all the generations of the future.

From *This is the American Earth*
by Ansel Adams and Nancy Newhall

Ansel Adams: GRAND CANYON, FROM THE NORTH RIM

Ansel Adams: EL CAPITAN, YOSEMITE NATIONAL PARK

Ansel Adams: YELLOWSTONE FALLS, YELLOWSTONE NATIONAL PARK

Gene Aherns: THE GENERAL LEE TREE, SEQUOIA NATIONAL PARK

LUTHER BURBANK
1849–1926

roamed as a boy in the fields and
forests of his native New England. He
loved the tangled fields of wild flowers
and the gentle green meadows of the
Massachusetts countryside. Luther
never lost his love of growing things or
his thirst to learn all he could about
them. A chance reading of a book by
Charles Darwin when Luther was
nineteen convinced him that plants
could be changed and improved—that
man could make "new creations" out
of the familiar plants in his garden.
Luther had found his life's work! First on
a small plot of land in Massachusetts
and then on his experimental farm in
Santa Rosa, California, Burbank
devoted the rest of his life to develop-
ing hundreds of varieties of new fruits
and flowers—living proof of Burbank's
genius and his determination to make
plants work for man.

Luther Burbank
Partner of Nature
by Doris Faber

1. Buttercups in January!

"Look what I found in the woods," Luther Burbank shouted to his younger brother. "You won't believe your eyes."

Lute came running across a snow-covered field toward the Burbanks' red brick farmhouse. A pale winter sun shone down on the Massachusetts countryside. It was a cold Saturday morning in January.

Alfred stopped tapping icicles from the porch. He ran to meet Lute.

The older boy's blue eyes beamed with excitement. He held out a small bunch of golden *flowers*.

"Buttercups!" Lute called. "Buttercups in January!"

Alfred tried not to seem disappointed. But what was so wonderful about a few flowers left over from summer?

"Where did you get them, Lute?" Alfred asked without much interest.

"Down in the hollow beyond the pines," Lute cried. "It's spring down there, it really is. There's not a sign of snow on the ground. Just the greenest grass you ever saw. Come on!"

Alfred caught some of his brother's excitement. Together they set off across a field of hard packed snow.

Soon they walked by the frozen pond. Here they skated in the winter, and swam and fished in summer. Then they passed the sugar maples. Next month the boys' father and older brothers would make small holes in these trees. They would hang buckets beneath each hole. Drops of sweet sap would fall in the buckets. The sap would be boiled till it turned into wonderful maple syrup. Lute's mouth watered at the thought.

At last they were in the deep, still, wintery woods. Snow covered the carpet of pine needles. Tall trees were black against the white snow. Suddenly Lute pointed ahead. There was a gap among the trees. Sun was shining on the ground below. There the boys saw bright green grass.

Alfred shook his head. Lute certainly had a way of discovering things. It was like magic.

"Why do you think—" Alfred started.

"I'm going to try to find out," Lute said.

He slid down the last snowy slope. Reaching the

grass, he sank onto his knees. He put his mittens into his pocket. He touched the earth.

"It's warm," he said, "much too warm to let the snow stay. But why?"

Alfred shook his head helplessly.

"Grass and flowers aren't *supposed* to grow in January," Lute said, frowning. "How can they?"

Lute thought a minute. "I'll ask Cousin Levi!" he said. "I'm glad he coming over this afternoon."

Years later, Luther Burbank's name was known all over the world. He had grown hundreds of new kinds of fruit and flowers. But even when he was an old man, he remembered the day he found buttercups in January.

That day started him on the road to fame, he said. That day he saw one of nature's tricks. Then he asked questions till he understood it. And he began to learn how to be a partner of nature.

2. Cousin Levi

The rich smell of apple pies filled the Burbank kitchen. Lute's big sisters were helping Mrs. Burbank fix supper. Lute stood near the kitchen fire with Cousin Levi.

"Now what's this about buttercups?" Cousin Levi asked. "I think that's interesting."

Cousin Levi had read more books than anyone Lute knew. Lute's own father was a great reader when his farm work was done. Like many New England families, the Burbanks loved learning. But nobody in the whole large family had as much learning as Cousin Levi Sumner Burbank.

Cousin Levi worked at a Boston museum. There he studied unusual rocks. They helped him learn what the world had been like many years ago. He also knew about other kinds of science.

Lute told him where the buttercups were growing.

"Ah!" said Cousin Levi. "I know the spot. There is a warm spring of water under the ground at that place. The warm water keeps the earth near it warm all winter."

"Are there many springs like that? How does the water get so warm?"

As Lute was asking questions, the door opened. His father and brothers came in from the barn. They stamped their cold feet before the fire.

"What's this lad asking about, Levi?" Mr. Burbank said. Then he smiled at Lute. Mr. Burbank loved all his children. But Lute was special in one way. Mr. Burbank had eight older boys and girls who were almost grown. Their mother had died. Then Mr. Burbank married again. Lute was the oldest child in this new family.

"Luther asks good questions," Cousin Levi replied.

"He's always asking questions," Mrs. Burbank added fondly.

Lute felt shy at all this talk about himself. But he still wanted to know about that warm spring. He looked up at Cousin Levi hopefully.

"There are many springs like that," Cousin Levi said. "Warm rocks deep under the earth heat the water."

"About the buttercups," Lute said, forgetting the others were listening. "Can they keep on growing? Can the same plants keep on making new flowers winter and summer?"

"I don't think so," Cousin Levi said. "Buttercups will bloom for only a few weeks. Then they will drop tiny seeds for new plants the next spring. Your buttercups were just hurried along. The warm water must have fooled them. They thought it was spring already."

Lute nodded excitedly. "I see!" he said. "It would be fun to get some other seeds. Then I could fool some other flowers into growing with the buttercups."

"Fooling plants!" Lute's father shook his head. "Don't be a foolish boy, Luther."

Cousin Levi smiled at Lute. "You help your father, lad," he said. "You'll learn a lot from him, and from your schoolwork. But I'll teach you too. We'll take some walks in the woods together."

3. Searching

"You ought to go to college, Luther," Cousin Levi said.

"But we don't have enough money for college."

The boy and the man were walking through the woods. For five years, they had been taking long walks every time Cousin Levi came to visit. Now, in 1866, Lute was fourteen.

"Let's rest on this rock," Cousin Levi said. He looked at his young cousin. He saw a thin boy, not very tall. The most unusual thing about him was his eyes. Those bright blue eyes never missed a fern or a bird.

"You should be a scientist, Luther," Cousin Levi said. "You have keen eyes and a keen mind. But you must go to college first to study science. If you need money, get a job for a few years. Earn money. Then go to college."

Lute felt warm inside. It was nice to be praised by a great man like Cousin Levi. And it *would* be exciting to be a scientist like him. Or maybe a doctor. Lute didn't like the idea of going to college, though. He enjoyed reading by himself, but he didn't like school.

One day soon after this, his teacher asked him to stay after class.

"What's your trouble, Luther?" the teacher asked. "Why don't you answer when I call on you? You do such good written work."

"I don't like to talk in front of all those boys," he said. "They laugh at me after school."

The teacher thought a minute. She knew Lute was shy. Sometimes he could not seem to talk clearly. She also knew he was small for his age, and poor at games.

"I understand," the teacher said. "From now on, I won't call on you in class. But be sure to hand me a neat paper every morning. I'm going to grade you on your homework."

Lute was so grateful that he worked extra hard on his homework. And he didn't really mind being teased after school by other boys. He liked to hurry home instead of hanging around to play ball the way Alfred did. At home he could try out the new ideas always buzzing in his head.

One day he took a small tin whistle. He tied it to his mother's teakettle. He put the kettle on the stove. When the water inside the kettle began to boil, it formed steam. The steam blew into the whistle. "Toot! Toot!" How his little sister Emma laughed!

Another time Lute took Emma to the pond. He had built a toy waterwheel there.

"Bring your doll," he said. "I can make her do a trick."

Lute tied one end of a string to the wheel. He tied the other to the doll's arm. Then he paddled with his hand to make the wheel turn. This made the doll wave to Emma.

All these ideas gave Luther's father an idea of his own.

"You ought to work in a factory, Luther," he said. "You think of so many little tricks. Who knows? You might think of some new sort of machine. In a factory that would be helpful. I don't see the use of it on a farm, though."

Luther was pleased that his father thought he might make a good workman. But he would hate to spend his life indoors. *What* could he be when he grew up?

He was still trying to find an answer when his father became ill. Luther was seventeen years old. All his older brothers had left home. They were married and had their own families. Somebody had to earn money to take care of his parents and the younger children.

Luther was not strong enough to run the farm by himself. So he took the first job he found. He went to work in a nearby plow factory.

4. Woodworking

"What are you doing there, Burbank?" Luther's boss asked.

Luther looked up, startled. But his boss, Mr. Ames, did not seem angry. He seemed interested.

"I thought I could work faster this way," Luther said.

His job in the factory was to make plow handles. A machine called a lathe turned the wood round and round while he cut and smoothed it. His pay was 50¢ for each plow handle.

Luther made fine plow handles by doing the job the way his boss had shown him. Mr. Ames was pleased with him. But Luther was not pleased himself. It took him a whole day to make one plow handle.

He thought over all sorts of ideas for doing the job faster. Why couldn't the machine do more of the work? That would speed things up.

So this evening he had stayed late in the factory. He was trying to fix his machine. He fixed it so it held the wood and cut and smoothed it too. Mr. Ames watched as Luther worked. Luther made a plow handle in only an hour!

"Amazing!" Mr. Ames said. "Why didn't somebody think of that before?"

Luther's pay went up and up after this. He made so many plow handles that soon he earned six or eight dollars every day. The money was a great help at home. And Mr. Ames was pleased to pay it.

"You have a great future here, Burbank," he said.

But Luther was not happy. The sawdust in the factory made him cough. He hated staying indoors so much. Sunday was the only day he had time to walk in the fields and woods he loved. During the week, he could hardly wait until evening came. Then he read books about plants. He got book after book from the village library.

"Here is a new book," the librarian said one evening. "I think you will like it."

This book changed Luther Burbank's life. It was *The Variation of Animals and Plants under Domestication.* It was written by the great English scientist, Charles Darwin.

"Darwin says plants can be *changed!*" Luther told his mother excitedly.

Luther knew already that most plants grow seeds. These seeds are grown in the pistil of the flower. They begin to form after the sticky top of the pistil, called the stigma, is touched by pollen.

Pollen is produced by every flower inside the anther, a part of the stamen. The tiny grains of pollen look like golden dust. Pollination takes place when the stigma is touched by pollen from its own flower or from another one.

"Darwin says a red flower can be pollinated by a yellow flower," Luther told his mother. "Then the seeds that form may grow orange flowers!"

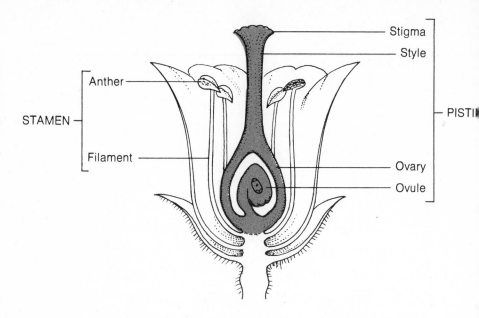

CROSS SECTION OF A FLOWER

"Is that so?" Mrs. Burbank asked in surprise.

"Yes!" Luther went on. "Insects and birds—and sometimes wind or water—carry pollen from one plant to another. But Darwin says *men* can do this too."

Luther's face grew thoughtful.

"Can men make *new* kinds of flowers this way?" he asked. "Could I make new flowers? Or fruit?"

Luther had found his life's work.

But nobody else thought it was a good idea to work at changing plants. Some scientists were trying tests with plants. But they did not plan to *improve* plants in a big, bold way. Luther Burbank did.

He still had to earn money, though. He could not leave the factory yet. It would be several years before he could begin his great work as a partner of nature.

5. Farmer Burbank

When Luther was nineteen years old, his father died. His older brothers said the family farm must be sold. Luther got a share of the money for the farm. He made up his mind to buy another farm and start on his great work.

"I want *to train plants to work for man*," he told his mother.

"But you're not strong enough to be a farmer," Mrs. Burbank said.

"I won't need a big piece of ground," Luther said. "I don't even know exactly what I'll do yet. But I have to try."

Mrs. Burbank shook her head. Luther's older brothers tried to change his mind. But he stood firm. He bought a farm not far from his old home. He used most of his money to pay for it. He had hardly a penny left. And he had no clear plan.

"But I have a hoe and a pair of overalls," he said.

His whole family thought he was foolish. Even his mother thought so. But she and Emma came to keep house for him.

Luther had nobody to ask about his ideas for experiments with plants. He did not know about the slow, careful tests some scientists were making.

"I'll just grow a little corn and some beans this year," he told his mother. "I can sell them in Boston. I can get some money that way. And I will read more books. Then maybe I can try some tests."

Again Mrs. Burbank shook her head. She had lived on a farm all her life. She knew it was not easy to make money growing vegetables. There were many other farmers with more experience than Luther had.

Luther knew this too, but he had an idea. He remembered the buttercups he had once found in January. He would *fool* his corn into growing faster. He planted corn seeds indoors. The seeds grew quickly in warm, indoor boxes.

In May, other farmers planted corn seeds in their fields. Luther had small, healthy corn plants to set out in *his* field. He had ripe ears of corn two weeks before the other farmers. He had no trouble selling them.

That was Luther Burbank's first small success. He had helped nature to hurry. He could have gone on growing vegetables for Boston stores for the rest of his life. He would have become known among his neighbors as a good farmer. But he had too many other plans.

6. A Great Potato

"I want to move to California," Luther told his mother. "It's warm all year there. I could grow fruit there that won't grow here. I could work with plants all year round."

Mrs. Burbank sighed. "That's so far away."

"Oh, I can't go yet," he said. "I don't have money for a train ticket."

Mrs. Burbank sighed again. Three train tickets would cost three times as much. She and Emma would have to stay at home with some other relatives. And Luther would go off by himself. She knew he would. He would manage to do it somehow.

And he did. Luther found a way for a potato to pay his way to California.

One day Luther was in his potato field. He saw a plant that looked a little different from the others.

What Luther saw on the potato plant was a small seed ball. He knew how unusual this was. He knew that potatoes were not like most plants.

To grow potatoes, a farmer cut an old potato into several small pieces. He made sure each one had an eye. He planted them in the ground. Then green leaves would grow up above the ground. In the fall, the farmer would dig up the potato bush. Growing with the roots, many new potatoes would be found.

These potatoes were just like the potato he had cut up and planted.

Only once in a great while would a potato plant grow a seed ball. The seeds in it were different from most seeds. Potato seeds do not grow new plants just like their own parents. They grow all sorts of strange and often useless potatoes. But Luther was excited by his discovery.

"I may grow a new kind of potato with these seeds," he told his mother.

His tiny seed ball had 23 seeds in it. All winter Luther kept these seeds cool and dry. Then the next spring he planted them in a special bed.

Even Mrs. Burbank was excited. She watered the 23 special plants for him. Emma helped to weed them. Mrs. Burbank and Emma watched eagerly when the day came to dig up the special plants.

Luther pushed his fork into the ground. Up came the roots of the first plant. He shook his head.

Mrs. Burbank said nothing. The small round potatoes she was used to cooking were much better than these. Poor Luther!

Luther pushed his fork into the ground again. Again and again he dug up a few ugly potatoes. At last there was only one plant left. Luther pushed his fork into the ground unhappily. The fork would not come up. Was it stuck under a rock?

Luther pushed the fork till it finally came out of the ground. Suddenly his eyes opened wide. That was no rock it had caught! That was the largest potato he had ever seen! And there were twelve more like it on this last plant.

In the kitchen, Mrs. Burbank washed the huge potato. She popped it into the oven. Finally it was cooked. She cut it into three pieces.

"Don't burn your mouth!" she warned. Luther didn't listen. Emma didn't either.

"It's the best potato I've ever tasted!" Emma said.

Luther Burbank had found the famous Burbank potato.

To this day, many of the large baking potatoes we eat are Burbank potatoes. For Luther saved the other twelve potatoes through the winter. Then he cut them in pieces and planted them. He did this for three years. Then he had a big bag of Burbank potatoes. He sold them to a man in the seed business for $250. Soon there were thousands of Burbank potatoes to sell to farmers as seed potatoes. But even before this Luther Burbank was on his way to California.

7. A New Start

In California Luther settled in the town of Santa Rosa. This was almost sixty miles from San Francisco.

The hills were ripe with wild poppies. The wild grapes were the sweetest Luther had ever tasted.

"This is the chosen spot of all this earth as far as nature is concerned," Burbank wrote to his mother. "The air is so sweet it is a pleasure to drink it in."

What if he were 26 years old and penniless again? Burbank loved California from the day he arrived.

He worked as a carpenter to earn a little money. He did odd jobs at fruit ranches. He earned enough to buy a small plot of ground near the edge of town.

"I'm going into the seed and plant business soon," he told new friends. Some wondered if he would do well at it. He seemed to spend most of his time walking about the sunny hillsides.

"Look, these are poppy seeds," Burbank told a farmer he was working for. Burbank showed him a bag of tiny black seeds.

"But who would want those?" the farmer asked. "Poppies grow wild. You don't plant them."

"They grow wild in California," Burbank said. "But where I grew up, people have never seen a poppy."

"Well, poppies wouldn't grow in that cold country anyway," the farmer said.

Burbank smiled. "You may be right," he said. "But I'm going to send some of these seeds to my mother. She'll try them for me."

Mrs. Burbank did try them. She wrote good news

to Luther the next summer. She had a patch of golden poppies growing in her Massachusetts garden.

Burbank went to a printer in town. "I want you to print some cards for me," he said. "I'm going into the seed and plant business."

"What are you going to call your nursery?" the printer asked.

Burbank thought a minute. "Just say I'm 'The Nurseryman South of the Iron Bridge,'" he said.

The Nurseryman South of the Iron Bridge started his business with his shoe-strings. He did not have enough money to buy many plants and seeds to sell

Burbank wandered in the high Sierras, selecting wild flowers and gathering seeds.

to farmers. But he did have his keen eyes and his shoe-strings.

He walked about the hills looking for wild flowers. He took along strips of white cloth to tie on plants with the finest flowers. Often he ran out of cloth and used pieces of his shoe-strings. Then in the fall he went back and looked for his markers. He gathered seed from the plants he had marked.

California people did not buy much from him at first. But he wrote to seed men in Massachusetts and other states. They were interested in trying California seeds. Soon the Nurseryman South of the Iron Bridge was mailing seeds all the way to England!

8. 20,000 Prune Trees

Burbank had been in California six years. His nursery business brought him a little money. But he was far from rich. He still had to work as a carpenter now and then. He had little time or money to try plant tests. Then one spring day a man came to see him at his cottage.

"I want to go into the prune business," the man said. He was Mr. Warren Dutton, a banker. "I want 20,000 nice, big prune trees right away."

"I'm sorry," Burbank said. "I don't have a single prune tree."

Prune trees were new in California then. Someone had brought the first one from France only a few years before.

"There is a lot of money to be made in selling prunes," Mr. Dutton said. "After the prunes are dried in the sun, they will keep for months. I can sell them to people as far away as New York. I would be willing to pay you well for the trees. I heard you have some new ideas about growing plants. Nobody else has been able to help me. I hoped maybe you could."

Burbank thought for a minute.

"Maybe I can!" he said suddenly. "Come back tomorrow. I will let you know then."

Burbank was excited by Mr. Dutton's idea. But could anyone make nature hurry as fast as Mr. Dutton wanted it to? That night Burbank thought of a plan. Now he had a chance to try an important experiment.

"I will have the trees for you by December," Burbank told Mr. Dutton the next day. "They will be good sized trees. You will have some fruit from them next summer."

"That sounds like magic," Mr. Dutton said. But he did not really believe Burbank could keep his promise. Nobody did.

The first thing Burbank did was to buy 20,000 *almond* nuts.

Burbank planted the almonds in a bed of sand. Soon

green tips began to show. Burbank moved each baby tree to a field where it would have more room. Soon he had a field of strong young almond trees.

Then he went to a neighbor who had a few big prune trees. From him, Burbank bought 20,000 prune *buds*. Burbank hired several men. Soon he and his men were starting an amazing job.

All fruit growers knew it was possible to graft a piece of one tree onto another. This meant setting a shoot or bud from one tree into a cut in another tree so as to grow there.

HOW TO MAKE A BUD GRAFT

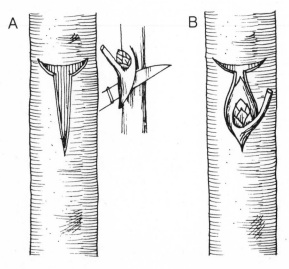

A cut is made through the bark of a tree and the edges of the bark are raised.

A bud is removed from another tree and inserted in the cut.

The bud is wrappe tightly to the tree wi tape or string.

First, a cut was made through the bark of the tree and the bark edges were raised. Then a shoot or bud with a small portion of bark was cut from another tree. The shoot or bud was pressed tight to the tree. It was tied or wrapped to hold it in place till it began to grow in its new home.

Some grafting was done by all fruit growers. But never before had it been tried on so many trees at once. Burbank was the first man to think of mass-producing trees this way.

Burbank and his men grafted prune buds onto every almond tree. After the buds started to grow, he broke off the tops of the almond trees and let them hang so that all of the strength of the tree went into the prune bud. The new wood that grew was prune wood. Burbank had changed the almond trees into prune trees. In December, he sold Mr. Dutton 19,500 strong prune trees.

"You are a magician!" Mr. Dutton said.

9. Red Plums

Mr. Dutton paid Burbank well for the prune trees. Now more farmers came to buy from the Nurseryman South of the Iron Bridge. Now Burbank had earned enough money to bring his mother and Emma to California.

"Here are two train tickets," Burbank wrote to his mother. "Please come with Emma as soon as you can."

When they arrived, they found him excited about a book he had just read. It was written by an American sailor who had been to Japan.

"Look!" Burbank said. "He found a new fruit in Japan, a big, sweet, juicy *red* plum."

"But plums are small and black," Emma said.

"They make good jam," Mrs. Burbank said. "But they are too sour to eat raw."

"These Japanese plums must be different," Burbank said.

He had sent California poppy seeds to a seed man in Japan. Now Burbank wrote to this man. He asked him to ship twelve small Japanese plum trees to California. The trees arrived in the spring. Burbank planted them and tended them carefully. One tree produced big, sweet, juicy red plums.

Burbank grafted buds from this tree onto many other trees. Soon fruit stores began to sell sweet red *Satsuma* plums. That was the name Burbank gave his fruit.

He used the other Japanese trees for tests. These were the kind of tests he had dreamed of trying.

"What are you doing?" a fruit grower asked him.

"You want plum trees that will give fruit early in the season," Burbank said. "You want trees that will grow well in warm, dry weather. You want fruit that can travel miles to market."

The grower nodded.

"Another man wants late plums," Burbank explained to the fruit grower. "He wants trees that will live through cold winters. You both want strong trees that will not die of disease. And every mother wants sweet, juicy fruit for her children. I am trying to help nature help all of you."

Every day Burbank worked at his tests. He took a healthy tree that gave sour fruit. He brushed its flowers with pollen from a tree that gave sweet fruit. He tried to *combine* the good things about both trees in order to develop a better fruit. He made thousands of tests like this.

He also grafted buds by the thousands. He started every spring with long rows of test trees. He let them grow only a few months. Then he *selected* the best ones.

"Why are you burning good trees?" a farmer asked him.

"They aren't good trees," Burbank said. "They'll never have good fruit."

The farmer asked for some of the trees anyway. He planted them. He did not graft buds and hurry nature along. He waited six summers until they had fruit. The fruit was small and ugly.

"I didn't believe you," the farmer said. "Those trees looked all right."

Burbank smiled. "I can't explain it," he said. "But I can tell with one look if a tree is worth saving."

He surely could. By now he had trees growing pretty red plums and green plums and yellow plums. So he *selected* again.

"Here, Susie," Burbank would call to a little girl who lived across the road. "I want you to taste this plum. I think you will like it even better than the ones I gave you last week." Many children were glad to help him by tasting plums.

And his mother cooked big pots of jam for him.

"This batch is best," Emma said.

"Fine!" Luther said. He made a note on a piece of paper.

Some plums passed all the tests. Then Burbank used his prune tree trick. He made thousands of new trees quickly. He sold them to fruit growers all over California. He even sent many to South America and Africa and Australia.

10. Fame

Burbank's hair began to turn white. His mother died, and Emma got married. Now he lived alone again except for his friendly dog, Bonita.

Burbank at work in his garden—pollinating a poppy (above) and exhibiting a new variety of the flower

But he had many visitors. Newspapermen came miles to write stories about him.

"Luther Burbank works magic with plants," they wrote. "He has developed ten new apples, sixteen new blueberries, ten new cherries."

In time they counted almost 250 new fruits. There were many new vegetables, too. He developed a green pea sweeter than any then known. He developed sweeter corn. He even tried to "train" cactus plants to grow with smooth leaves.

Cactuses are plants that grow in hot, dry places. He thought these could make good food for cattle. But they had sharp needles on every leaf. After many years, Burbank grew some cactuses without needles. But rabbits ate them before the cattle could! This was one of Burbank's few failures.

But he had wonderful success with growing flowers.

"Burbank roses smell sweeter than others," newspapermen wrote. "His lilies have stronger stems and bigger blooms than other lilies. He has 'trained' golden California poppies to grow red or purple flowers. He has tamed wild daisies."

Newspaper stories brought hundreds of people to see for themselves. They looked over his fence. Many begged to come in.

"I don't have time to stop my work," Burbank

would say. But often he stopped anyway. Whenever a group of children came, he stopped.

"Would you like some juicy cherries?" he asked them. "Would you like to see a daisy as big as a dinner plate?"

Every year on his birthday, dozens of Santa Rosa children came to visit. They sang "Happy birthday to you" on his doorstep. The small, gentle man with the silvery hair loved to listen to them.

He was honored by many famous visitors too. The king of Belgium came. Great scientists came. Burbank would not take time off from his work to travel. Still he met many of the great men of his day.

11. Indian Summer

Burbank kept working like a young man. Every day he walked through his grounds to see how his plants were doing.

For several years now, Elizabeth Waters had been his secretary. She kept plant records for him, as Emma had before her marriage. Elizabeth was a cheerful and bright-eyed young woman. At the age of 67, Burbank married her. She brought her ten-year-old niece, Betty Jane, to live with them.

The little girl loved to play with Bonita, Burbank's friendly dog. Together they romped through the house. Burbank's hair was snow-white by this time, but he loved to play too.

"Folks wonder how I've kept so young," he said. "I can still go over a gate or run a race. That's because my body is no older than my mind. My mind has never grown up. I'm still as full of questions as I was when I was eight."

Burbank's shoulders were bent from long years of garden work. But he never stopped planning new plant tests.

"There is still so much to do," he said. "I hope many children who love plants will carry on my work. I must do as much as I can, though."

Some scientists did not think Burbank's work was as wonderful as newspaper stories said. They did not trust him because he had not studied science in college. They thought he did not keep careful records.

Some other people disliked him. He had let careless friends sell Burbank plants. Sometimes they sold new plants before they were ready. The farmers lost money when the plants did not grow properly.

But most people admired and loved him. Burbank's great idea of "training plants to work for man" was no longer laughed at. Many other men were working on plant tests too.

In 1926, when Luther Burbank was 77, he became very ill. A few days later he died. Plant lovers

Here in Luther Burbank's workroom, the brilliant naturalist is surrounded by the seeds and roots of his plant "creations."

everywhere were sad. But Burbank had done what he set out to do. He said before he died: "I shall be contented if, because of me, there shall be better fruits and fairer flowers."

Plant lovers today can enjoy these fruits and flowers. They can grow them in their gardens. And they can walk through Burbank's own test gardens. The city of Santa Rosa turned these into a nature museum. Every year, thousands of people go there to see where Luther Burbank did his great work as nature's partner.

The American Earth: A Priceless Heritage

The proud mountains and dense forests of America
have been disfigured
- by the plunder of our natural resources
- by junked and rusting cars
- by carelessly discarded "throw-aways."

The clean-flowing waters and the beaches they wash
have been polluted
- by oil spills from tankers and drilling operations
- by chemicals from farms and factories
- by raw sewage from cities.

But land can be restored and waters cleansed, if we but have the will. Science and technology have a role to play in finding new and better ways to protect our environment. And we, working together, can help
- by cleaning up oil spills
- by picking up litter
- by using our resources wisely

and by caring enough to provide a clean and beautiful earth for Americans still to come.

RACHEL CARSON
1907–1964

became America's conscience in the
1960s in the long, uphill fight to protect
the environment against dangerous
chemicals. For as long as Rachel could
remember, she had loved the land and
the sea. She loved to write too. At
college Rachel reluctantly took a
required class in biology in her junior
year that changed the direction of
her life. She embarked on a course of
study that would earn her a degree in
biology. Then at the Marine Biological
Laboratory on Cape Cod, Rachel finally
saw the ocean for the first time! She
was never again to leave it for very
long. Rachel Carson combined her
talent for writing with a career as a
marine biologist. Her books about the
teeming life that inhabits the ocean and
its shores made the gifted writer-
scientist a national figure. Then in 1962,
Rachel Carson lashed out at the use of
chemicals and pesticides which were
poisoning the earth. Her book, *Silent
Spring*, stirred Americans into caring
about their environment and taking the
first painstaking steps to protect it.

Rachel Carson
Who Loved the Sea

by Jean Lee Latham

1. Tagalong

A gentle hand shook Rachel. Mama whispered, "Rachel, dear."

Rachel opened her eyes. It was dark. "What's wrong?" Then she remembered. "Oh, yes. Today is special, isn't it?"

"Very special," mama said.

Soon mama led the way with a flashlight across their yard and into the dark woods. She and Rachel sat on their favorite log. Mama switched off the light.

"When will they begin to wake up?" Rachel whispered.

"Any minute now."

Rachel heard a sleepy little twitter, then another one. "Hello, birds," she called softly. "And good-bye! Summer is over. I can't play here all day anymore. School begins in two days!"

Now all the birds were singing.

"It's just like they were talking back to me, isn't it? I wonder how many birds we have?"

"Goodness knows," mama said. "We have over 50

acres of woodland. There must be thousands and thousands of birds."

"And they all talk to me." Rachel sighed. "I guess people don't understand about that."

"What do you mean, dear?"

"Ladies down at the store are always whispering behind my back, saying 'poor little lonesome girl.' What's lonesome?"

"That means you're sad when you're alone. The ladies just think you are alone a lot because our place is out from town."

"But I'm not sad. And I'm not alone! I have all the woods and the birds and the rabbits and—and—everything! I'm not lonesome."

"I know. I think you're lucky. I think we're all lucky to have all this lovely woods, only 18 miles from Pittsburgh." She got up. "Time to get breakfast."

For a moment Rachel stood looking up into the trees, smiling. "Good-bye, birds." The bird songs followed them all the way to the house.

After breakfast Rachel's big brother Robert said, "You want to go to the store with me?"

"Oh, yes!"

Papa said, "Remember, Robert—"

Robert grinned. "I know. It's more than half a mile to Springdale. My legs are long. I mustn't walk too fast."

As they went down the hill Robert asked, "Did you tell the birds good-bye this morning? Tell them about school?"

"Of course. The little new ones wouldn't know."

"You're a funny youngun," Robert said, "but I guess I like you anyhow." Then he began to ask crazy riddles, and they laughed all the way to the store.

But when they started home from the store, Rachel was very quiet. What had the ladies meant? She knew they had been talking about her.

"What's got your lip out?" Robert asked.

"Nothing." She smiled at him. "Do you know any more riddles?"

"Of course."

She thought about the riddles and tried to forget the ladies.

That afternoon mama made ginger cookies. Rachel sat on a high stool by the kitchen table. What had the ladies meant?

Mama took a pan of cookies out of the oven. "As soon as they're cool, you may have one."

"I'm not hungry."

Mama dusted off her hands and felt Rachel's forehead. "No, no fever. What's wrong, Rachel?"

"I'm not hungry."

Mama just waited.

"Mama, what is a 'poor little tagalong?'"

"My goodness, where did you hear that?" said mama.

"Down at the store. One lady said, 'Carson's poor little tagalong.' Is it something bad?"

"Oh, no, no! It just means that you are lots younger than the others. Robert was ten and Marian was eight when you were born."

"It's all right to be a tagalong?"

"Of course. Don't give it another thought."

Rachel picked up a cookie. For a minute she sat looking at it. Then she said, "But I wish the ladies wouldn't say 'poor little thing' about me all the time!"

2. Rachel Makes Up Her Mind

Robert tiptoed up behind the chair where Rachel was sitting. "Boo!"

Rachel jumped and dropped Robert's magazine, *St. Nicholas.*

Marian said, "Robert, don't you know better than to scare a lady when she's reading?"

"She wasn't reading," Robert said. "She was staring off across the room. What were you daydreaming about?"

"Nothing." Rachel smiled and gave Robert his magazine. "Here."

"No, keep it."

"Thank you!" Rachel went up to her room with

St. Nicholas. She opened it again to her favorite part, The St. Nicholas League. It gave the names of all the girls and boys who had sent stories to *St. Nicholas.* The best stories were printed in the magazine with the name of the author.

If only she could think of a story. If only there could be a story with "written by Rachel L. Carson" on it. Then the ladies would not "poor little thing" about her all the time, would they?

For a long time she sat and stared. Somebody called, "Supper!" She sighed and went downstairs.

"I wonder," she asked papa, "where writers get ideas for stories?"

"I've heard they get them out of newspaper items sometimes," papa said.

But Rachel did not like to read the newspapers just then. In 1916 World War I was going on in Europe. Everything in the paper was about war.

Rachel was glad the war was on the other side of the ocean. She had never seen the ocean, but she knew about it. It was big—bigger than anything else in the whole world!

"I'm glad the war is clear across the ocean," she said one night. "It won't come over here, will it?"

Papa sighed. "We hope not."

Marian said, "But papa, President Wilson is keeping us out of the war."

"He's doing his best to keep us out." Papa got up. "Come on. Let's sing."

Mama smiled and went to the piano.

Sometimes Rachel sang with them. Sometimes she shut her eyes and listened. Everybody said they had beautiful voices.

For a while they sang together. Then mama began to play one of Rachel's favorite songs, "Rocked in the Cradle of the Deep." Papa always sang it alone in his deep, rumbly voice.

When the song ended, Rachel gave a big sigh. Songs and poems about the sea were the best of all. Someday she would see the ocean.

She got up without a word, kissed them all good night, and tiptoed upstairs. If she didn't think about anything else, she might dream about the ocean.

By the spring of 1917, Rachel didn't want to dream about the ocean. America was in the war. Submarines sneaked through the ocean and blew up ships.

She missed Robert. He was in the army, learning to be a flier. Every week he wrote a long letter home. How they all gathered around to hear mama read it!

One letter told about a brave English flier. He had been in fierce battles. Now he was in the United States to train American fliers.

"I'll bet he's glad he can help win the war without getting shot at anymore!" Robert wrote.

The next day another letter came from Robert—a very thin one. The brave young English flier had been killed in an accident.

Rachel went up to her room. She got out her tablet and pencil. She started to write, stopped, crossed out the words, and started again. It was hard to make a story say what you felt. Three times she started over again.

At last the story was done. She made a fresh copy. She showed it to mama. "Is it good enough for *St. Nicholas?*"

"I think so!"

"Thank you!"

When the next copy of *St. Nicholas* came, Rachel grabbed it, opened it in a hurry, and turned to the St. Nicholas League. Her story was not there.

"They haven't had time to print your story yet," mama told her.

"How long will it take?"

"Two or three months. Maybe longer."

"And maybe," Rachel said, "they never will print it."

"They must get hundreds of stories, Rachel."

Long months passed. Summer came and went. School began again. One day Rachel opened the September number of *St. Nicholas.* She turned slowly to her favorite part. She jumped up, shouting, "I did it! I did it!" There was her story in print, with her name: Rachel L. Carson.

And there was a letter for Rachel with a check for ten dollars. She made up her mind. "When I grow up, I'll be a writer!"

3. Cash Money

Now Rachel began to think about the stories mama read them in the evenings—especially the stories about the sea. How could anybody ever learn to write like that?

She had started high school when she asked, "Mama, how can I learn to be a real writer?"

"First, read all the good books you can. Next, practice writing."

"I do that now!" Rachel said.

"Then, get a good education."

"High school, and then college?"

"Maybe some education after four years of college."

"What else is there?" Rachel asked.

"College people have special names for how much education you have. When you are through college, you have a bachelor's degree. Then you may take special work and get a master's degree. You may even take more work and get a doctor's degree."

"I don't want to be a doctor."

"It doesn't have anything to do with medicine. It just means you are very, very educated. You are called a doctor of philosophy."

"I just want to be a writer."

"Then the first thing is to make good grades in high school, so you'll have a chance to go to college."

"Why?"

"Because we have more land than 'cash money.' Papa keeps hoping to sell some land for building lots, for people to put houses on. But right now people aren't buying. So—well—it takes a lot of money to go to college."

"How much?"

"I'd like to see you go to a college in Pittsburgh —Pennsylvania College for Women. It costs about $1,000 a year. Sometimes colleges give scholarships to bright students who need help. That means the college pays part of the bills for a student with a good record."

"So that's why I'll need good grades—to get a scholarship."

"Yes, dear. Unless times get better, you'll need a scholarship to go to college."

All through high school Rachel worked hard at every subject, whether she liked it or not. By her senior year, she had a long record of high grades.

"We're proud of you!" mama said.

"It's easy to make top grades in English," Rachel said. "But, oh, that science! I've had enough science to last me the rest of my life."

"You'll find college more interesting. You'll settle down and take extra work in what you like best. In college they call that your major."

"I know what my major will be." She wished she could be in college right now. Another half year of high school, then summer vacation. More than six months before she could go to college—if she got a scholarship.

Her English teacher came to see mama. "You want Rachel to go to Pennsylvania College for Women, don't you, Mrs. Carson?"

"Yes," mama said. "We've written to them, but we haven't heard yet."

"I've written to Miss Cora Coolidge, the president of the college," the teacher said. "I've told her about Rachel. Not only top grades, but she has a real gift for writing."

Mama smiled. "Thank you! I'm sure that will help."

When the teacher had gone, Rachel hugged mama. "I'll get it! I know I'll get it! I wonder how much it will be? Maybe $500? Or maybe the whole $1,000?"

"We'll just have to wait and see."

At last a letter came from the college. Rachel's fingers shook as she opened it.

The college was glad to accept Rachel L. Carson as a student. It would give her a $100 scholarship.

4. What's Come over You?

Only $100! How could she ever get the other $900 she would need for even one year of college?

"If I can just get started," Rachel said, "I'll work so hard that—that—well, something will *have* to happen!"

Papa scraped together all he could. He'd send her more later, he said, even if he had to borrow it.

When Rachel got to the college, she asked to talk to Miss Coolidge. She told her how things were.

"As mama put it once, 'We have more land than cash money.' Is there any work I can do to help pay my way through college?"

Miss Coolidge shook her head. "I'm sorry, Rachel. The only thing I can suggest is—do your best and hope for the best."

"I certainly will!" Rachel said.

She often spent her weekends in the library, reading. She spent many long evenings studying and writing.

She took part in everything that had anything to do with writing. She worked on the college newspaper. She sent stories to the college literary magazine. Month after month, her stories were turned down. Finally, at the very end of the year, one of her stories was printed.

Some of the girls said they enjoyed it. "You lucky girl!" one said. "You can just dash off something I'd have to work a month to write."

Just dash off something! Rachel smiled to herself. If they only knew how many times she wrote even one sentence over and over again. But she was learning. Next year she would keep on learning. By the end of next year. . . .

Then she found out a sad fact.

Before she could graduate, she had to have some work in science. What a waste of time! Silly work in a laboratory, looking at bugs through a microscope. Just a lot of crazy words to learn—words that she could never use in a story!

Well, she might as well do it, and get it over with. She'd take biology. All the science majors said Miss Mary Skinker was a wonderful teacher. "She works you like a dog," one said cheerfully, "but what a teacher!"

In September Rachel sighed and walked into her first biology class.

Mary Skinker greeted her with a warm smile. "I read your story last spring, Rachel. I'm so glad to have you in my class."

This picture of Rachel appeared in her college yearbook.

"I'm sure glad one of us is glad," Rachel thought.

But after the class Rachel walked down the hall in a daze. What a teacher! Miss Skinker really did make biology interesting.

Biology was the study of life—everything that lived. One part—botany—was about all the trees and plants and flowers. The other part—zoology—was about all the animals and birds and fish. Biology was about everything!

After a month Rachel began to feel like two people. One Rachel was making top grades in English and having stories in the college magazine. The other Rachel was thinking about biology—all of life.

Once she started thinking about biology in English class.

"Rachel Carson," she said to herself, "what's come over you?"

The middle of Rachel's third year, her teachers said it too: "Rachel Carson, what's come over you?" Rachel had changed her major to science.

Even Miss Coolidge sent for her. "Rachel, my dear girl, do you realize what you'll be going through your last year?"

"Yes, Miss Coolidge. At least six classes in science."

"But your wonderful gift for writing, Rachel! You do have that. We have expected you to graduate magna cum laude."

Rachel knew what that meant: Cum laude was "with honor." Magna cum laude was "with great honor."

"We have hoped we could get you a full scholarship to work on your master's degree. Please, won't you think about it?"

"I have thought about it, Miss Coolidge. I know I want to work in science the rest of my life. In biology."

Miss Coolidge just shook her head sadly. She didn't argue any longer.

Only Miss Skinker was pleased. "I'll miss you next year, Rachel," she said, "but I know I'll be proud of you."

"You'll miss me?" Rachel asked.

Miss Skinker was going to Johns Hopkins University to work on her doctor's degree.

5. Two Jobs at a Time

Her last year Rachel began work in six classes in science. All the girls but the science majors were fussing at her. Why had she thrown away her chance to be a great writer? What chance was there for her in science?

Rachel did not bother to argue. She did not have time to argue. She was working harder than she had ever worked before. In October she had a letter from Miss Skinker.

"As the girls used to say, 'They are working me like a dog,' but it's a wonderful school. I hope you can come here someday."

Not much chance of that, Rachel knew. She would be in debt when she finished college. Nothing but a full scholarship would help her go to a university to get her master's degree.

Another letter came from Miss Skinker. She was sick. She had had to give up her work at Johns

Hopkins. But she still hoped Rachel could go there someday.

In the spring Miss Coolidge sent for Rachel. What was wrong? Rachel could remember that talk last year, when she changed her major to science. She could still see Miss Coolidge shaking her head.

Miss Coolidge was shaking her head again, but she was smiling. "Rachel, you amazing girl!"

Rachel was graduating magna cum laude—with great honor. She had won a full scholarship to work on her master's degree at Johns Hopkins. And that was not all! In August she would go to Woods Hole, at Cape Cod, Massachusetts.

"You will meet great scientists from all over America," Miss Coolidge said. "Woods Hole is the home of the Marine Biological Laboratory—where men study the life of the sea."

Rachel blinked back tears. She could not keep her voice from shaking. "Oh, Miss Coolidge! I've always dreamed about the ocean. But I've never seen it."

"You certainly will this summer, my dear."

One morning in August she stood on the deck of a boat, speeding toward Woods Hole through choppy waters. Again she blinked back tears, though she was smiling. The ocean! How long she had dreamed of it. Now she was on it. She could see it and smell it and feel it as it beat against the boat.

For the six happiest weeks of her life, she studied at Woods Hole. She met men of the U.S. Bureau of Fisheries. She went out with them in a boat as they studied the ocean.

"This is what I want to do someday," she said. "I want to work in the Bureau of Fisheries."

The men smiled. "We don't have women scientists in the Bureau."

"Maybe someday you will," she said.

They shrugged. She might talk to Elmer Higgins in Washington about it. He was one of the men in charge.

"I'll do that very thing," she said.

Before her classes started at Johns Hopkins she went to see Mr. Higgins. She told him what she wanted to do. He was a friendly man. He said there weren't any women scientists in the Bureau. But he wished her luck at Johns Hopkins.

Miss Skinker had been right. They did "work you like a dog" at Johns Hopkins. But Rachel's letters home were cheerful. She didn't say anything about the long, hard days. She didn't say anything about "no place for women scientists."

Mama's letters were cheerful too. She and papa were alone now. Marian was married, and Robert was working in Pittsburgh. They missed Rachel, but they were very proud of her.

Late in October the stock market crashed. Hundreds of men lost all the money they had. Banks failed. Factories closed. Thousands of men were out of work. The Great Depression had begun. Rachel knew that hard times had hit Springdale too. She felt she should do what she could for her family.

She found a house that she could rent very cheaply. It was out from Baltimore, but she could take a bus to Johns Hopkins. She wrote mama about it. They would have lean times anywhere. They might as well be together.

Papa found work sometimes in Baltimore. It didn't pay much, but it helped. Rachel got part-time work too. Some of her jobs meant long bus trips back and forth. Sometimes she thought she spent half her life going and coming.

All through her work at Johns Hopkins, Rachel did two jobs at a time. After three years she had her master of science degree in marine zoology—the life of the sea.

But the Great Depression was still going on. Rachel could not find a place for a woman scientist. There were only part-time jobs and long bus trips.

The summer of 1935 papa died suddenly.

At first Rachel could think of only one thing—how she would miss him. Then words seemed to hammer in her head: "You've got to earn more money!"

6. Fish Tales

Once more Rachel went to see Elmer Higgins in Washington. He listened; he rubbed his chin. Then he surprised her. "Can you write?"

Rachel had to laugh. "You should have heard the fuss when I changed my major to science." She told him about college.

"A scientist who can write. I may have a job for you for a few months."

The Bureau of Fisheries was doing short stories for a radio program. "It's called 'Romance under the Waters,'" he said.

"What a lovely name," Rachel said.

"We just call them the 'Seven Minute Fish Tales,'" he said dryly.

Mr. Higgins had a problem. Several people had tried to do the stories. The writers were not scientists. The men who were scientists could not write.

He gave her samples of the Fish Tales they had done. He gave her subjects for three more. "Take these home and see what you can do. If you can write them, you'll have a job—for a while. It pays about $20 a week—as long as it lasts."

Rachel smiled all the way home. That night right after supper she started on the Fish Tales. At last she stopped, looked up, and listened. It was almost dawn.

The birds were waking up! Smiling, she went out and leaned against a tree.

"Hello, birds," she called softly.

Presently all the birds were singing.

"Just as if they are talking back to me," she thought. She smiled at the memory.

When Mr. Higgins read her Fish Tales, he nodded. "You have the job. You may work at home or here in our library."

Sometimes Rachel worked at home. Often she worked until the birds woke up. Sometimes she made the long trip to Washington and worked all day in the library.

One evening when she got home, she stopped outside the door and listened. Who was typing so fast? Mama could type, but not that fast. She opened the door quietly and went in. "Mama!"

Mama laughed. "Oh, fiddlesticks! I wanted to surprise you when I got really good."

"You're really good now. You are amazing."

"What's amazing about it? I know—'You can't teach an old dog new tricks'—but I'm not 70 yet."

Soon mama was making all the final copies of the Fish Tales. "This is such fun," she said. "I hope it lasts a long time."

But Rachel knew it would not.

She heard there was to be an examination for junior

aquatic biologist. Marine biologists knew the life of the sea; aquatic biologists would have to know the life of both the sea and the rivers.

She thought back over the years. "If anyone has worked harder or learned more," she told herself, "I'll eat my hat!"

"I hear you want to take the examination?" Mr. Higgins said. "You'll probably be one in a thousand —the only woman."

"I know, Mr. Higgins."

When Rachel went to take the examination, she was the only woman.

The man in charge said, "Yes, young lady? You have something for me?"

"I'm here to take the—"

"What! I thought you were a clerk, with a message for me."

"No, I'm a scientist." Rachel smiled. "A woman scientist."

That evening mama was eager to hear all about it. How soon would Rachel get the job?

Rachel had to laugh. "You're sure I'll make the highest grade?"

"Of course," mama said. "How long before you'll hear about it?"

"Goodness knows." She went back to work on the Fish Tales.

One day Rachel went to the library in Washington.

A clerk said, "Oh, Miss Carson! Don't bother to sit down. Mr. Higgins wants to see you right away."

Rachel's heart sank. Was it the end of the Fish Tales? Was she out of work again?

7. Mr. Higgins Says No

Mr. Higgins came to meet her and held out his hand. "Congratulations! You are now a junior aquatic biologist. And I've asked to have you work for me. How's that?"

"Wonderful!"

"For a while you'll have two jobs."

"I've done that before."

"And you'll be here in the office most of the time."

More long bus trips. But Rachel only smiled. She was a woman scientist!

Her regular job, he said, would be to answer special questions people asked.

"Some questions can be answered with a booklet. Others can't. Those questions will be your job. If you know the answer, good. If you don't, you'll hunt till you find it."

"Yes, sir, Mr. Higgins."

"And we're going to bring out a book of the Fish Tales. I want you to write an introduction for it."

That Friday evening Rachel wrote her introduction to *Romance under the Waters.*

Mama read the introduction and looked up with shining eyes. "Why, it's beautiful! To think of writing something beautiful about fish."

"About the sea," Rachel said. "I think Mr. Higgins will like it."

But Mr. Higgins said, "No, Miss Carson. This isn't any introduction to our Fish Tales. It's a very fine article. Write another introduction for me. Send this to a magazine. You might try the *Atlantic Monthly.*"

A fine chance to have something in the *Atlantic Monthly!* Rachel put away her article and wrote another introduction to the Fish Tales.

Then she settled down to answering the questions in letters. Sometimes the days seemed very long.

When she got home, she always stopped outside the door, put on a smile, and then opened the door and called cheerily, "Anybody home?"

One evening mama did not answer. What had happened? "Mama!"

Mama was sitting in a chair, white as a ghost. "Marian is dead."

"Oh, no!" Then Rachel thought of Marian's little girls—just in grade school.

Mama said, "Marjie and Ginny—"

"Yes, they'll need a home."

Rachel found a house in Silver Spring, near Washington. She could be home more. She would not have to travel so far.

She sent for the girls. Would she know them? She had not seen them since they were little. Children changed so fast.

She knew them as soon as she saw them. Marjie looked so much like Marian.

"Rachel!" they shouted and came running.

Then her arms were full of two sobbing little girls. She didn't try to talk. By the time they left the station, they had dried their tears and were staring, big-eyed, at the sights.

The house in Silver Spring was a happy one. Mama sang as she baked cookies and smiled when she helped with lessons.

A home took money to run, though. And Rachel knew she had to earn more. She started writing articles for the Sunday magazine section of the Baltimore *Sun*. They didn't earn much. But even fifteen dollars helped.

She wished she had time to write the kind of things she'd like to do. But she could not write all night and sleep in the morning. When she had written the first introduction to the Fish Tales, she had worked till the birds woke up.

She read it over again. Yes, it was good. She made

a few changes and had mama make a fresh copy. She sent it to the *Atlantic Monthly.*

In six weeks a letter brought a check for $75. "Undersea" would be published in September 1937.

She didn't tell Mr. Higgins about it. She waited till she had the magazine. She opened it to "Undersea" and put it on his desk. Wouldn't he be surprised?

But in a few minutes it was Rachel who was surprised. "What did you say?"

"I said," Mr. Higgins told her, "that you ought to write a book."

8. Three Jobs at a Time

"Write a book!" Rachel gasped. "When would I write it?"

"You've got the heart of a book right here. Every paragraph in this article can be expanded into a chapter. And you'll have a book. Just like that."

Just like that! Did everybody think a writer just dashed off things?

"No, thank you, Mr. Higgins!" She had had enough of two jobs at a time.

But two letters came that changed her mind. Quincy Howe, editor of Simon and Schuster, wrote. Was Miss Carson writing a book on "Undersea"? His company would like to see it. Hendrik Willem van

Loon wrote. Mr. van Loon was one of the greatest writers in the world! Surely Miss Carson was doing a book? Mr. van Loon asked.

Rachel knew she was going to do it. But how? And when? How long would it take? A year? Two years? Two years of two jobs at a time?

There were weeks in the next years when she did three jobs at a time: her government work, work on the book, and articles for the *Sun*.

A dozen times in 1939 she thought of giving up. She was so tired. Why did she keep on?

"Just stubbornness!" she told herself. But she knew it was more than that. She was writing about what she loved, so other people could love it too.

Before the end of 1939, another war was raging overseas. World War II had begun. Rachel remembered when America had entered World War I. Then the ocean had not been a wonderful place to dream about. It was where submarines sneaked around and blew up ships. She used to have nightmares about the ocean.

If she ever dreamed anything now, she did not remember. She just worked and wrote and fell asleep —if she was not too tired to sleep.

Early in 1941 mama typed the last pages, and Rachel mailed *Under the Sea Wind* to Simon and Schuster.

"How will you celebrate?" Marjie asked Rachel.
"If I had time, I'd sleep a week," Rachel told her.

In November 1941 *Under the Sea Wind* was published.

The first book reviews thrilled mama. The *New York Times* said: "It promises its readers knowledge and sound enjoyment." The *Herald-Tribune* said: "There is drama in every sentence. She rouses our interest in the ocean world and we want to watch it."

Mama smiled. "It makes it worth all the work, doesn't it?"

"Almost. . . ."

Then the great Dr. William Beebe wrote, praising the book. He wanted to include two chapters in *The Book of Naturalists.*

Rachel took a deep breath. Yes, maybe it had been worth it. But it would be a long, long time before she'd work that way again.

On December 7, 1941, the Japanese attacked Pearl Harbor. World War II had come to America. War news wiped everything else from people's minds.

The book that had taken three years to write was forgotten in three months.

"Never again," Rachel said.

All through the war, new discoveries about the ocean came to Rachel's desk. Sometimes as she read, she would feel a tingle go up her spine. Nothing in

"Cry of shore bird and crash of surf were the sounds
of the edge of the land—the edge of the sea."
From Rachel Carson's *Under the Sea Wind*, 1941.

153

the world was so mysterious as the ocean. If only she had more time. . . . No! Not another book!

She was busier than ever with her work. The Bureau of Fisheries became the Fish and Wildlife Service. Now she studied the migrations of birds. She visited many wildlife refuges.

By 1948 she was editor-in-chief of books of the Fish and Wildlife Service. She had an office of her own, with five people working under her—even men. She had to smile at that.

By 1948 the wartime secrets of the ocean could be published. Rachel read everything she could find. At last she sighed and shook her head.

"Here I go again!" She was going to write another book.

She decided she'd get a literary agent to help her.

A young friend in Washington recommended Mrs. Marie Rodell.

⋅ "Of course, she is a woman," he said, "but she's got a fine reputation."

"A woman scientist shouldn't object to a woman literary agent," Rachel said.

She soon found out how much help a good agent could be.

In 1949, long before the book was done, Marie Rodell had a contract with Oxford University Press. But Oxford wanted the manuscript in ten months!

9. Time Enough

"I can't possibly finish it in ten months," Rachel said.

"Why not get a leave of absence from your job? Take time off?"

"I can't afford to."

Marie Rodell smiled. "You've heard of foundations, haven't you?"

"Guggenheim, Ford—that sort of thing? Yes. I know they make grants to colleges."

"The best thing they do with their money is to make grants to writers who are working on really important books."

Rachel wrote to Dr. Beebe about it. "A sound idea," Dr. Beebe said. He and Edwin Way Teale, the famous naturalist, both knew and admired her work. They would be glad to put in a good word for her. Soon she had a grant from the Saxton Memorial Fund.

She had enough money to take time off, but it was not so easy to walk out of her office. She took a month off—then found double work piled up and waiting for her when she got back. Oxford had wanted the book by February. It was July of 1950 before *The Sea Around Us* went to them.

Not long after that, Marie Rodell had sent her a

special message. Houghton Mifflin wanted Rachel to write a guidebook about the life of the seashore.

"Oh no!" Rachel said.

"We'll get a grant that's big enough for you to take a whole year off."

A whole year just to write? Rachel signed the contract.

"But I don't have a deadline," Rachel told mama. "They'll get the book when it is done. Now I can rest in peace. Oxford and Marie Rodell are taking care of *The Sea Around Us.*"

"What else is there for Mrs. Rodell to do?" mama asked.

"She wants to sell parts of the book to magazines to be published before the book comes out."

"Won't that hurt the sale of the book?"

"She says it will help. And she knows her business."

A chapter of the book came out in *Yale Review.* It won a $1,000 prize for the best magazine science writing of the year.

Then the *New Yorker* wanted to do three parts of the book. Of all things! It was a smart "citified" magazine. It printed "Profiles"—stories about famous people. Now it would do "Profile of the Sea." And the price made mama gasp.

The *Reader's Digest* offered $10,000 to do the book in a short form for their condensed books.

Meantime, Dr. Beebe and Mr. Teale were "going to bat" for Rachel. A grant of $4,000 came from the Guggenheim Foundation. In June of 1951 Rachel began her leave of absence for a year. A whole year to do nothing but study the seashore and get ready to write the next book!

Rachel celebrated by going to a beach she loved. A whole year of enough time and peace!

In July *The Sea Around Us* was published. That was the end of lazy days at the seashore.

The Sea Around Us was on the best seller list of the *Times,* and was a Book-of-the-Month Club selection. By Christmas time it was selling 4,000 copies a day.

Marie Rodell persuaded Oxford to publish *Under the Sea Wind* again. The book that had been forgotten in 1941 was on the best seller list in 1952. Two books by one author were on a best seller list at the same time!

Rachel gave back the Guggenheim grant. She resigned from her job. Now she had money and time to write anything she wanted to write.

But she found it took a lot of time to be famous. There were phone calls and letters. There were speeches to make and books to autograph. She had to be honored at receptions, luncheons, and dinners.

"I have money enough," she thought, "and I'll have time enough as soon as I get done being famous."

When Marie Rodell read the first chapters of *The Edge of the Sea*, she said, "You're going to have another best seller."

"Please, not that!" Rachel said. "I have another book I want to write."

10. It's Up to You!

In 1955 *The Edge of the Sea* was published. Marie Rodell had been right: a Profile in the *New Yorker*, weeks on the best seller list, Book-of-the-Month Club, and *Reader's Digest* condensed books.

Rachel was glad when summer came and she could go to Maine. It was her favorite place in the whole world.

Marjie and Ginny were both married now. Marjie was a widow with a little son. From the time Roger was two, he trotted along with Rachel to the woods and the beach.

Early in 1957, when Roger was five, Marjie died.

Mama said, "What will become of Roger?"

"I'll adopt him," Rachel said. "I am closer to him than anybody else."

"I'll help all I can," mama promised.

Mama was very crippled with arthritis now, but she could still read poems and stories as she had when Rachel was a little "tagalong."

Rachel was deep in plans for the next book, but Roger was never lonesome.

Now and then Marie Rodell reported that some magazine had offered a huge fee for an article.

"Tell them NO! The book I'm working on will take five years; the next one I want to write will take another five. And nobody, but nobody, is going to change my mind."

Early in 1958 she got a letter with a newspaper clipping from Mrs. Olga Owens Huckins, a long-time

Rachel Carson at her typewriter. The writer-scientist was still to make her greatest contribution to mankind.

friend. Planes had sprayed their region with DDT to kill mosquitoes. She had written to a paper:

> The "harmless" shower bath killed seven of our lovely song birds outright. . . . The next day three more were scattered around the bird bath. (I had emptied it and scrubbed it after the spraying BUT YOU CAN NEVER KILL DDT.)

Please, Mrs. Huckins wrote, would Rachel find someone who could stop this dreadful killing?

Rachel tried. She wrote a dozen letters. Then one answer jolted her: "Rachel Carson, you are the one person in the world to do this! A scientist who can write! *It's up to you!*"

"I'll write a brief book," she said.

She began to collect the facts. The grim reports poured in. A cold chill crawled through Rachel.

Those "wonderful, magical" pesticides were the deadliest thing man had ever spread on the earth. More reports came. Soon Rachel was sending out hundreds of letters all over the world.

She knew now it could not be a brief book. It was going to take more time to collect all the facts than any book she had ever done.

Those facts had to be right. She knew she was

going to have a fight on her hands. Pesticides were "big business." Big chemical companies were making millions of dollars out of them.

"I'll help all I can," mama said. But in December, she died.

For weeks Rachel was numb with sorrow. How could she go on? But she had to go on. She could not forget those words: *"It's up to you!"*

Her days had three parts now: "Readin', Ritin', and Roger." Even though she had a good housekeeper, Roger needed her time. How often he ran in, calling, "Rachel! Look what I found!"

And why was she getting so tired? Why did she feel so draggy?

During the spring of 1960, she went to Washington to see her doctor. "Find out why I am so tired, and put me back in shape. I have work to do."

Doctors operated. It was a tumor, they said, but not a cancer. She ought to be feeling fit very soon again.

But she did not feel fit soon again. Even with a fine secretary, she could never get enough done.

She sent a sample chapter of the book to a long-time friend who was a scientist.

"You're doing a magnificent job," he told her. "But I doubt it will be a best seller. You'd better be ready for quite a battle."

"I won't care if I do have a fight on my hands,"

she said. "The more they rave, the more people will read. *I'll do this book if it's the last thing I ever do.*"

Late in 1960 she found out it would be just that— the last book she would live to write.

11. The Last Book

The doctors finally told her the truth. She did have cancer. They could not get it all when they had operated. Now it was spreading. Yes, they said, they could give treatments.

"Just so I can keep on working," she said. "And one thing—"

"Yes, Miss Carson?"

"I'm going to say I have arthritis. People don't dither at you so if you say you have arthritis. I will not have people dithering over me."

Day after day, week after week, the work on the book went on. Fact after fact proved what man was doing to his world: poisoning the air, the earth, the water; killing birds, fish, and man himself.

The idea for the name of the book, *Silent Spring*, came from a poem by Keats:

The sedge is wither'd from the lake
And no birds sing.

Rachel finished the book early in 1962. It would be

published in September. But *Silent Spring* made headlines long before September. The Profile started in the *New Yorker* in June.

It shocked the nation. For the first time most people knew of the danger of DDT and other pesticides.

Letters poured in to Rachel, to the magazine, to Washington.

The chemical companies fought back. They spent thousands to try to prove that *Silent Spring* was just a silly thing by "that hysterical woman, Rachel Carson." As one newspaper said it, "*Silent Spring* became a noisy summer."

CBS asked Rachel if she would be willing to face her accusers on a television show.

"Nothing could please me more," Rachel said.

CBS announced that "The *Silent Spring* of Rachel Carson" would be seen on April 3, 1963. For months before the date CBS worked to do the show and put it on tape.

An odd thing happened. Letters poured in to CBS about a show that had not been seen. "Don't do that show!" But CBS did do the show.

Rachel watched it at home in Silver Spring and was glad. The book had been on the best seller list. Thousands of people had read it. But millions of people had seen the television show.

That summer she went to Maine. She knew it would

At the ocean's edge in Maine—a last look at the "shining beauty" of the mysterious sea

be for the last time. Roger, a sturdy little eleven-year-old, raced and shouted and found things and brought them to show to Rachel. It was a good summer. If only it could last longer.

She lay with binoculars and watched the flights of the birds to the south. She stayed until autumn made the trees a blaze of color. She watched one last moonrise over the water. Then she said good-bye to Maine and went back to Silver Spring.

One night in April she told her nurse, "I want you to waken me at 5:30 tomorrow morning."

"But, Miss Carson, it won't be light yet."

"I know. And I want you to wheel me out in the yard under the trees."

In the morning a hand shook her gently. "Miss Carson, you said to waken you."

"Yes! It's very special."

Rachel held the flashlight as the nurse wheeled her out into the yard. "This is fine. Thank you. I have the bell. I'll ring when I want you."

Rachel switched off the flashlight and sat in the dark. At last she heard a sleepy little twitter, then another, and presently all the birds were singing.

"Good-bye, birds," she called softly. "I'll not be around long. But I hope you'll be here for a long, long time."

She died on April 14, 1964. A service was held in Washington Cathedral. Senators, congressmen, and government officials were there to honor her—and many people who knew her only through her books.

Legend has it that Lincoln once said to Harriet Beecher Stowe, "So you are the little lady who started this big war."

Rachel Carson was the little lady who started another war—the fight against the careless use of deadly chemicals.

Index

education of, 134, 135, 136, 137, 138–139, 140, 141, 142, 143
father of, 130, 131, 134, 136, 142, 143
and Fish Tales, 144, 145, 146, 147, 148
great-nephew of, 158, 161, 164
and Guggenheim Foundation, 157
illness of, 161, 162
mother of, 126, 127, 128, 132, 133, 134, 135, 142, 143, 145, 148, 156, 158, 161
nieces of, 148, 149, 153, 158
and love of the ocean, 131, 141
and Saxton Memorial Fund, 155
as a scientist, 142, 144, 146, 147
and Silver Spring, Maryland, 149, 164
and U.S. Fish and Wildlife Service, 154
at Woods Hole, Massachusetts, 142
writings of,
    Edge of the Sea, The, 158
    Romance under the Waters, 148
    Sea Around Us, The, 155, 156, 157
    Silent Spring, 162, 163
    "Undersea," 150
    Under the Sea Wind, 151, 153, 157
Carson, Robert (brother of Rachel Carson), 127, 128, 131, 142
Coolidge, Cora, 135, 136, 139, 141

D

Darwin, Charles, 99, 100
David, Jacques Louis, 16, 17
DDT (chemical pesticide), 160, 163
"Death of a Glacier, The" (Muir), 72
Dutton, Warren, 108, 109, 111

E

Edge of the Sea, The (Carson), 158
Environmental problems, 120-123 (pics)

F

Fish Tales, 144, 145, 146, 147, 148

G

Glaciers, 61, 68, 70, 76, 77
Grand Canyon, 83
Grafting (plants), 110 (diagram), 111, 112
Griswold, Milton, 62

H

Havell, Robert, Jr., 35, 37
Hetch Hetchy Valley, 83
Higgins, Elmer, 142, 144, 146, 147, 148, 150
Huckins, Olga Owens, 159–160

J

Johns Hopkins University, 140, 141

L

Lizars, W. Home, 34, 35
Loon, Hendrik Willem van, 150–151

M

Marine Biological Laboratory, 141
Mountains of California, The (Muir), 81
Muir, David (brother of John Muir), 48, 49, 50, 51, 52, 53, 64, 66, 81
Muir, Helen (daughter of John Muir), 79
Muir, John, 47 (pic), 73 (pic)
    as author, 65, 72, 79, 81, 83
    moves to California, 67
    childhood of, 48, 49, 50, 51, 52
    and conservation, 72, 73, 80, 81, 83
    death of, 83
    education of, 52, 54, 57, 61, 62
    and father, 50, 51, 52, 54, 57, 60, 62
    at Fountain Lake Farm, 52, 53
    and glaciers, 61, 62, 68, 70, 72, 75–78